REAL DOGS
DON'T
Eat Kibble!

SANDRA BAILEY

BOOK ONE of *The Naturally Healthy Dog Series*

Creative Genius

An Imprint of Morgan James Publishing • NEW YORK

REAL DOGS DON'T Eat Kibble!

The Naturally Healthy Dog Series™

Copyright ©2008 Sandra Bailey

ISBN: 978-1-60037-301-5 (Paperback)

Published by:

Creative Genius

An Imprint of
Morgan James Publishing, LLC
1225 Franklin Ave Ste 32
Garden City, NY 11530-1693
Toll Free 800-485-4943
www.MorganJamesPublishing.com

Cover/Interior Design by:
Rachel Campbell
rachel@r2cdesign.com

Contact Sandra G. Bailey at:
http://www.thenaturallyhealthydog.com
Email: info@thenaturallyhealthydog.com

Habitat
for Humanity®
Peninsula
Building Partner

DEDICATION

TO ALL THE DOGS I HAVE LOVED in the past …
Lady, Smokey, Button, and Phoenix,

To my one cat that I rescued at three days of age
and who contributed to my life for 16 years …
Gimlet,

To the dogs that I happily share my life with now…
Digit, Pip, and Squeeze,

And to my Mom and Dad, Nila and Stokley Bailey,
who always supported my love for animals and
taught me to respect all living things.

CONTENTS

Foreword   *vii*

Introduction   *xiii*

CHAPTER 1 No Healthy Dog?   1

CHAPTER 2 Why Raw Food?   19

CHAPTER 3 Foods to Use   37

CHAPTER 4 Food to Avoid   69

CHAPTER 5 Putting It Together: Recipes and Portions   77

CHAPTER 6 When You Can't Feed Fresh Food   99

CHAPTER 7 The Importance of Journaling   125

CHAPTER 8 Looking Ahead   141

CHAPTER 9 Conclusion   151

CHAPTER 10 Forms   157

About the Author   *163*

Rainbow Bridge   *166*

Appendix   *169*

Photo Acknowledgements   *171*

Contact Information   *175*

Bonus   *177*

"This is important information that every

dog guardian should read."

—CHRISTINE M MULLEN

⚒ FOREWORD ⚒

AS A BREEDER WHO HAS RAISED and bred Papillons

for over thirty-six years, my dogs' well-being is as important

to me as my own. I began my dogs on the natural raw food

Ch. SunBelt's Calamity Call with her daughter SunBelt's Caret

vii

diet over fifteen years ago when one of them had pancreatitis, and the difference in the health and appearance of my dogs now and the dogs I bred earlier is **miraculous**. I have every belief that the raw natural diet is the major contribution to this change.

Sandra takes a subject of which many dog guardians are not aware, and writes it in language that is easy to understand. The emphasis of the book is on prevention of illness. As you read, you'll realize that her passion and love for ALL DOGS, not just her own, led her to write this book.

She is very clear as to why this food plan is needed and is the best nutritional diet that you can have for your dog. She points out how varied it is and how easy it is to put together.

Your dog deserves for you to read this book. It is clear that Sandra has all dogs' best interest and health at heart. If you feel the same way, then you need to buy this book.

To long life and good health for your dog,

Christine M. Mullen

SunBelt Papillons

Ch. SunBelt's Euro

"God bless the first man to kiss a wolf!

He opened the door for the rest of us!"

—Sandra G. Bailey

⇜INTRODUCTION⇝

I'M SURE THAT FOR ALL OF US, the well-being of our dogs is very important. I know that for me, they are my furry, four-legged children. I have had dogs for over fifty

Digit at 3 months - in the snow

years and at the present, I have three Papillons. Previous to that I had two Papillons over a span of twenty-six years. My first one, Button, died at a young age of nine years and I was determined to have the second one, Phoenix, for twenty years.

So, that is when I started looking at other alternatives to treatments and diet. Phoenix was treated homeopathically from the beginning, and I don't think she had antibiotics more than five times in her life. She was a beautiful tri-colored Papillon who I showed to her Championship. The veterinarian I was using at that time was beginning to study homeopathy and traveling to England in order to do so. She told me not to be afraid of antibiotics, but to keep them in reserve to use when they were really needed.

At that time, not many breeders were using a raw diet, but were preparing their own cooked diets for their dogs. I did the same and as a result, my precious Champion Benjerbo Phoenix, was active and alert for seventeen years.

When I received Digit four years ago, her breeder had been feeding the raw diet for over fifteen years and I have embraced the raw diet and plan to have my "girls," Digit, Pip, and Squeeze, with me for many years. I am very close to my dogs, and because they are a toy breed, they are with me all the time. This gives me the opportunity to watch them closely, be able to have fun with them and at the same time observe their health.

I felt compelled as a dog "guardian" to write this book as an introduction for dog lovers who would like to have more information on the Raw Diet and alternative health care. I also want to introduce you to a "system of observation" to follow and a journal to help you along the way.

I will always stress diet as the starting point. It is the foundation of good health and the first line of defense against disease. Fresh food is the first step. A varied diet of fresh meats, fruits, and vegetables may require a little more time to prepare, but is well worth the effort in the long run.

When we fall in love with our dogs, we know that there are only a limited number of years that we will have them. This book is written for all of us who want to increase the quality of those years, and along the way, have the happiest, healthiest dogs possible.

We are their guardians and it is our duty and privilege to make their lives the best possible while we are blessed to have them.

Sandra G. Bailey

Ch. Benjerbo Phonix

"**WE NEED ANOTHER** and a wiser and perhaps more

mystical concept of animals.

Remote from universal nature,

and living by complicated artifice,

man in civilization surveys the creature

through the glass of his knowledge

and sees thereby a feather magnified and

the whole image in distortion.

We patronize them for their incompleteness,

for their tragic fate of having taken form

so far below ourselves.

And therein we err, and greatly err.

For the animal shall not be measured by man.

In a world older and more complete than ours

they move finished and complete,

gifted with extensions of the sense

we have lost or never attained,

living by voices we shall never hear.

They are not brethren;

they are not underling;

they are other nations,

caught with ourselves in the net of life and time,

fellowprisoners of the splendour and travail of the earth."

—HENRY BESTON

"Dogs are not our whole life,

but they make our lives whole."

—Roger Caras

"I don't believe we really know what a healthy dog or cat looks like these days. We can only speculate."

—DON HAMILTON, DVM

☙ CHAPTER ONE ❧
No Healthy Dog?

American Rat Terrier – Nipper

That is the statement that compelled me to write this book. Dr. Hamilton also states that pets are not living as long today as they did sixty years ago. Are things really that bad for our pets? If a veterinarian makes

1

statements like that, then what do we as pet guardians know? Better yet what can we do? What does it take to have a naturally healthy dog?

In my introduction, I stated that for over twenty years now, I have been doing everything I can to add to the quality of my dogs lives. And I truly believe that I am on the right path, along with a number of veterinarians, breeders, and guardians.

The truth is, we are killing our dogs with medications and commercial processed food.

Veterinarians will tell you that very little time is devoted to studying nutrition when they are in school. Added to the problem is that most of them are courted by the major manufactures of commercial processed dog food and are told that their product is "complete and balanced." Fortunately some veterinarians have gone on to educate themselves about nutrition and many are also open to information from their clients. Today, just about every domestic animal has a chronic illness.

People have come to believe that their dog is suppose to have a strong "doggy" odor, bad breath, tartar on the teeth, eye discharge, wax in the ears, fleas and worms, anal sacs that have to be expressed and many other problems. The truth is that these are signs of chronic diseases and the dog is in a weak condition. The immune system is compromised and this leaves the dog at risk for more serious illnesses. These diseases can be thyroid, arthritis, lupus, diabetes, irritable bowel and even cancer.

When a veterinarian treats these conditions with medications, it suppresses the expression of the disease and actually adds to the deterioration of the dog's health. The risk of acute illness has been traded for levels of chronic illness. To eliminate the symptom without curing the underlying disease, will make the body even sicker, because the illness will look for another way to express itself.

So, what can we do to make sure that our dogs live a long and good quality life? We can educate ourselves as much as possible on the subject in order to understand why this has happened. We can learn what is natural for our dogs to eat and why. We can pay more attention to what our dogs are telling us and we can take notes along the way.

Given the chronic diseases that are affecting our dogs today, the first step is to prevent them from occurring. It is much easier to prevent an illness than to cure it. Promoting the health of your dog will be the best choice in the long run. This is supported by proper nutrition and lifestyle. Good nutrition is based on a species appropriate diet. A healthy lifestyle consists of fresh air, sun, and exercise.

The fact is that our dogs are carnivores and we need to look at their evolutionary past and their natural diet. Diet is the place to start and understand why it is important and why certain foods are called for. What is the right diet? We first have to look at the digestive system of the dog and what nature and evolution have done. How does their digestive system work and what is it designed to do?

Our canine friends have a digestive system that is designed to process raw foods. It has not changed over the millions of years that they and their ancestors have been around. As a species, the canine has been shaped by eons of evolution to eat specific foods. Their digestive system is short in order to process food quickly and they have enzymes and other natural chemicals that are needed to digest the specific foods that they have evolved to eat.

Even though we have domesticated them, internally they have not changed. They still have the same digestive system that their ancestors had those many years ago and if they had been left to their own, they would have followed the same diet.

Unlike humans, dogs do not produce stomach acids until they eat. With dogs being predators in the wild, they would gorge themselves on their prey and then rest between kills. This was an important benefit because it allowed the digestive system to clear and clean itself between meals. These cleansing periods are essential and it is important to feed your dog intermittingly to maintain good health. A healthy adult dog should only be fed once per day.

One of my friends couldn't believe that dogs are supposed to eat raw food. So, I said, "I want you to think back to the dawn of man, and as he looked upon the land around him, he observed a pack of wolves. He admired the way they worked together as they hunted and followed their prey, and just when the time was right, they sprang together and ripped open a bag of processed dry dog food...... Of course, this is why man has supermarkets today. That is how we learned to hunt." In other words just stop and think.

In the wild the canine family eats raw foods. They hunt prey and eat raw meat. They are "omnivores" and along with their prey, they like to eat raw vegetables, fruit, nuts, seeds, grasses, and berries. My dogs love to eat the acorns that fall in my yard. In the fall, it is much fun to watch them race each other to see who will get the acorn that just dropped.

That is where we as their guardians come in. We need to educate ourselves so that we can provide the proper foods that our dogs require. The ground work for this subject has been laid down for us over the past twenty years. Many breeders, veterinarians, and dog guardians have been using and have been successful with the raw diet. But before we look at raw food and why it is the best diet for our pets, let's look at commercial dog food and what it has done.

WHY OUR DOGS ARE NOT HEALTHY

A growing number of veterinarians are stating that processed pet food is the main cause of illness and premature death in the modern dog and cat. In December 1995, the British Journal of Small Animal Practice published a paper contending that processed pet food suppresses the immune system and leads to liver, kidney, heart and other diseases. This was researched further by the Australian Veterinary Association and proven to be correct.

Many studies have shown that processed food is a factor in increasing numbers of pets suffering from cancer, arthritis, obesity, dental disease and heart disease. We know that before WWII, most North Americans fed their pets raw bones and table scraps. Stop and think. What did people feed their pets before commercial processed pet food came onto the market?

I remember my grandmother throwing raw meat scraps, cornbread, biscuits, and leftovers out into the yard for the dogs and cats. Our relationship with dogs began 14,000 years ago and from that time until commercial dog food came on the market, we have shared our food with them. In most parts of the world today, people continue to prepare their dog's food.

The dog food industry did not exist until the 1940's, and the way it came about was companies trying to figure out how to make money from the "stuff" they had left over that was not fit for human consumption. That is how the pet food industry was born – how to make more money. Up until then, people fed their pets whatever they were eating and of course, the pets hunted small game and rodents and got the species appropriate diet that nature intended for them to have. They don't know any better – if left to themselves, that is how they would eat and that is how their digestive systems are designed.

For many years people have been drawn toward processed foods for the convenience, but diet is not the only thing that has changed for our pets. The life expectancy of many breeds is now less than half what it was three decades ago. Skin and coat problems in particular are so common today, that we accept them as unavoidable.

Today's veterinarians routinely treat some conditions that use to be rare and are now considered inevitable in some breeds. Chronic diseases, such as thyroid, cancer, arthritis, heart and liver disease, are not uncommon in our dogs today. These diseases are virtually unknown among animals in the wild due to the biochemical reactions that occur with their natural diet that strengthens their immune systems. This is available to your dog by using a natural diet.

WHAT IS IN COMMERCIAL DOG FOOD?

Overall, processed dog food is not good for your dog. The pet food manufactures choose products based on the least cost. You would think that looking at the label, and buying a food that list protein as its highest percentage ingredient would be the easy thing to do. But all protein is not the same. Some proteins are useful to your dog and others are not. This is particularly important when it comes to dry food. Not only are some of the proteins useless to your dog, their value is destroyed by high temperatures while preparing the product.

There are two sides to the problem of processed dog food. One is the point above, which supports the fact that nutrition is missing, and the other is that some ingredients are added that are dangerous. So, you look at what is missing that your dog needs and what is added that your dog certainly does not need.

Without going into detail, it is common knowledge that the undesirable remnants of the human food industry find their way into pet food. It stands to reason that if it is undesirable for human consumption, it can't have much value for the nutritional needs of your dogs. The USDA is not required to inspect the ingredients in pet food. Also, in all but two or three states, pet food manufactures are allowed to use tumorous tissues, hair, hooves, feathers, and animals that are dead, dying, disabled, or diseased when they get to the slaughter house. Some of these animals are dogs and cats that come from kill shelters and some of them have on flea collars and that also goes into the food along with the toxins and poisons in their bodies.

The manufactures can also use moldy grains or rancid animal fats. The meat scraps can contain hormone levels that have been known to cause cancer in lab animals and when the livestock is slaughtered for processing, the hormones are still active. Just stop and think about the fact that the cheaper the food, the more suspect its quality. Many veterinarians believe that these substandard foods and wastes increase the chances of dogs getting cancer and other degenerative chronic diseases.

Then there are the chemical additives in the food. Common ingredients that are added are propylene glycol, potassium sorbate, ammoniated glycyrrhizin, sucrose, propyl gallate, ethoxyquin, butylated hydroxytoluene (BHT), BHA, salt, and sodium nitrite. These ingredients are known to cause serious illness in dogs. Among these diseases are liver and kidney damage, cancer, heart disease, hypertension, thyroid disease, brain defects, nervousness, anxiety, diabetes, arthritis and others. Then you add the artificial coloring that does not require labeling. Some are possible carcinogens and others have shown in studies to increase dogs' sensitivities to fatal viruses.

In addition to the chemicals that are added to pet food, other chemicals enter in other ways. Herbicides, fungicides and insecticides are used in growing crops. These crops are fed to livestock who are also given growth stimulants, hormones, antibiotics, tranquilizers and other drugs. After the livestock is slaughtered and processed, more chemicals are added to preserve, soften and enhance the color of the meat.

Your poor dog has to eliminate the toxic substances and use energy and nutrients that are needed for other functions. If these substances cannot be eliminated, they accumulate in her body tissue and can interact with each other in harmful ways.

It is obvious to see that commercial processed foods are depleted of energy and nutrients and that there is a good chance for a toxic accumulation to occur in your dog's body. A dog's body has a detoxification method that was designed to deal with the natural poisons that it would come in contact with during its lifetime. But there is no way that it can overcome the thousands of chemicals that are being introduced today, and that includes the ones that are showing up in commercial processed dog food.

WHAT IS MISSING IN COMMERCIAL DOG FOOD?

Life energy! Qi! Or better known as enzymes. Enzymes are absolutely essential for every biochemical function of the body. Enzymes do not occur in processed foods, because they are destroyed by heat and processing. They only occur in raw food. That is why nutritionists tell us that raw fruits and vegetables are good for us.

Then there are many vitamins and minerals that are missing, or at least missing in the appropriate amounts. Even though they may be listed on the package, they may be unchelated which means they tend to pass right through the body and are not used. Also, they may be in incorrect ratios to each other.

NOW WHAT?

It is obvious that processed pet food is not the food that our dogs' bodies have evolved to thrive on through the millions of years that they have been here. And sixty years on processed dog food is not long enough to change their digestive systems.

Over the past sixty years, we have been overcome with processed foods, needless drugs and surgeries, pesticides, excessive vaccination and quick fixes that it should be clear to us that we are going backward fast.

I find it interesting that the same diseases that have developed in our pets over the past sixty years are the same diseases that have developed in man over the past hundred years. That is the period that man began to pump hormones and antibiotics into our livestock and began to use artificial fertilizers and insecticides on our crops, which we then feed to our livestock.

We just do not eat fresh livestock that was raised on fresh feed, and we do not eat fresh fruits and vegetables. Processed foods have created a mine field for us, and also our pets. Thank goodness many small farmers are beginning to raise organic fruits and vegetables and raising free range livestock.

So, let's get to the next chapter and explore Raw Food and why it is important!

"To create health,

you need a new kind of knowledge,

based on a deeper concept of life."

—DEEPAK CHOPRA, M.D.

☜ CHAPTER TWO ☞

Why Raw Food?

Basset Hound

Simply put, today's dogs are not doing well physically or emotionally. Veterinarians are seeing more immune system problems, genetic disorders and chronic diseases than ever before. Many of these problems and diseases are

19

caused by months and years of eating an inappropriate diet of commercially prepared foods. The build up of additives and dyes act as poisons and any nutrition that may have been present in the raw products was destroyed by the cooking process. A dog actually uses more energy to eat and process the food than the dog receives from the food in the first place. And then the liver, kidneys and pancreas has to deal with all the toxins. Each succeeding generation develops more serious health problems.

UNDERSTANDING DISEASE

First disease is broken into two categories - acute disease and chronic disease. **Acute diseases** are generally contagious and affect younger dogs. They usually affect the individual for a short period of time, although it is often intense and may even be life-threatening. Also, the symptoms are the same in all dogs that become affected, because the symptoms are associated with the infectious organism and not the patient. But once the patient recovers, the disease is gone and there is no re-infection and no lingering illness.

The beneficial effects of contagious diseases are that they strengthen the individual and enhance the immune system so that in the future the individual is more able to heal. In a group of individuals, acute diseases help to clear the group of weaker individuals, and improve the survival of the group. The use of vaccinations actually counters these forces by allowing the weakest of the group to survive and pass on its weak tendencies.

Chronic disease is everything else but acute, contagious disease. It is an inability of the body to heal itself, and the condition gets worse over time. All adult diseases are chronic. These are conditions such as thyroid disease, arthritis, cancer, diabetes, skin problems and many more.

Even if an individual is diagnosed with several conditions, they are just different expressions of the same illness. Only one disease occurs in the body, and that is the inability to cope with the stresses of life, both physical and mental, and it creates a weakness in the body. The immune system is suppressed, and this allows the organisms associated with chronic illness to infect the individual.

I will not discuss this any farther at this time, but do plan to address this whole issue in my next book. But for right now, the important thing is for you to understand the fundamental difference in acute and chronic diseases, and to realize that the majority of the conditions that affect our dogs are chronic and that the basis of that cause is a suppressed immune system.

You will want to know what you can do to strengthen your dog's immune system, so that he is better equipped to fight off disease naturally. The first thing you will want to do is to start your dog on the raw diet of organic, natural whole foods. Secondly, you will want to find a holistic veterinarian who understands what you are trying to do and will support you. If there is no one near you, they all do telephone consultations. And thirdly, you will want to allow any conditions that your dog has to express themselves naturally.

Your dog's body will always send a disease to an organ that it feels can handle it, and usually the first place expresses itself with the skin. With a holistic veterinarian, you will learn that you do not want to suppress these symptoms, but you will learn how to help your dog feel better.

HOW TO HELP BUILD AND MAINTAIN A HEALTHY IMMUNE SYSTEM

The immune system is a network of specialized tissues, organs, cells, and hormones. There are two main types of immunity. **Innate immunity** is a system built into the body to resist disease. **Acquired immunity** is the immune system's ability to adapt as the body comes in contact with pathogens through exposure, illness or vaccines.

SYMPTOMS OF A WEAK IMMUNE SYSTEM ARE SHOWN AS:

skin infections

recurring parasites

and mild illnesses that develop into more serious
health issues.

This occurs because the body's immune system is not strong enough to defend itself.

As I will always stress, diet is the starting point. It is the foundation of good health and the first line of defense against disease. Fresh food is the first step. A varied diet of fresh meats, fruits, and vegetables may require a little more time to prepare, but is well worth the effort in the long run.

It is important that your dog have a healthy gastrointestinal tract in order to get the most benefit from the raw diet. If your dog's system is weakened by allergies or digestive disorders, the nutrients even in a raw diet will be harder to process and absorb. Digestive enzymes, probiotics and essential fatty acids all contribute to your dog having a healthy system and proper digestion.

Two other contributors to a strong immune system are exercise and weight control. Exercise helps to build and maintain a strong immune system. Weight control is important because overweight dogs are more susceptible to chronic and acute infections and diseases.

ANTIOXIDANTS

An easy way to help boost the immune system is to use a good quality multi-vitamin and mineral supplement daily.

Antioxidants are important because they support the immune system and help rid the body of free radicals. Stress, poor eating habits, and environmental conditions can increase the amount of free radicals that attack the body on the cellular level, causing cellular malfunctions and some forms of cancer.

Free radicals are reactive compounds that are created in the body and are unstable because they contain extra energy. Because of this, they interfere with the cells ability to function normally. Antioxidants reduce the energy of the free radicals, stop them from forming, and minimize the damage that is done. Taking antioxidants can reduce the risk of free radical related health problems, such as cancer, aging, and a variety of diseases.

Although the body produces some enzymes that scavenge free radicals, it cannot manufacture the principle micronutrient antioxidants Vitamins A, C, and E. They must be supplied in the diet.

Vitamin A is found in the liver and other tissues. It is most abundant in the fish liver oils. Carotene is found in plant material and dogs can convert it into vitamin A with an enzyme that is found in the intestinal walls. Vitamin A makes white blood cells which destroy viruses and harmful bacteria which help regulate the immune system. Vitamin A helps the skin, mucous membranes, and urinary tract.

Vitamin C is manufactured in the liver and kidneys of dogs and is the most abundant water-soluble antioxidant in the body. Fresh fruits provide this valuable nutrient.

Vitamin E is in vegetable oils, cereal grains, greens, liver and eggs. It is the most abundant fat-soluble antioxidant in the body. It is very helpful in protecting against oxidation in fatty tissues

THE POTTENGER STUDY

A study was done in the 1930's known as The Pottenger Cat Studies. This study was performed from 1932 to 1942 under controlled conditions and involved 900 cats. Francis Pottenger Jr., M.D. separated cats into three main groups. They all received the same basic diet of meat, milk, and cod liver oil. The first group ate raw meat and raw milk. The second group ate raw meat and pasteurized milk. The third group had cooked meat and raw milk.

The cats that ate the all raw diet flourished and never needed veterinarian attention. The cats on the cooked diets became weak and malnourished. Their health problems were much the same as what vets see today – mouth and gum problems, thyroid disorders, bladder inflammation, allergies, skin problems, parasites, skeletal deformities, behavior problems and so on. Over a period of three generations, the cats that received the cooked diet continued to decline until they could no longer reproduce.

Dr. Pottenger also noticed that the plants that were in the pens with the cats on the all raw diet had lush growth. The plants in the pens with the cats on the cooked diet had spindly, poor growth. No Qi or energy from food to cats, so no Qi or energy from cats to plants. He then placed the first and second generation cooked-food cats on a raw food diet, and it took four generations for their line to recover from the ill effects of consuming cooked food.

This study proved the importance of feeding raw foods to animals, and that heat changes the molecular structure of food with a negative effect on heath. It also shows the destruction that inappropriate food can bring about over a period of time.

The other primary reason that our canine friends are not doing well is over-vaccination and over medication of conditions that make it appear to improve the symptoms, but in reality, drives the disease or condition deeper into the body. I do not plan to address the alternative treatments at this time, but do plan to pursue this subject in my next book.

SO, WHAT'S NEXT?

First things first, what is important now, is for you to know that these diseases and conditions can be avoided by maintaining a species appropriate diet, good water, exercise and care.

Most of the health problems in dogs stem from poor diet and nutrition. That is why it is so important to provide correct nutrition. With knowledge of fresh, wholesome foods, you can provide the proper nutrition for your dog. You will see an improvement in his condition, such as any allergies, skin, coat and ear problems, liver, kidney and bladder infections, fleas and parasites, as well as digestive troubles. If you are lucky to have a dog that is currently healthy, you will also notice a change in the quality of her coat, the brightness of her eyes, her general overall appearance and her level of energy. What a gift to give her!

The old saying is true – you are what you eat. If you eat poor quality food, your digestive system will bear the consequences first. The same is true for your dog. The organs that become affected are the liver, pancreas, kidneys and skin. The liver and pancreas are affected as part of the digestive system and the liver, kidneys and skin as part of the elimination system.

Fresh foods provide the healthiest source of nutrition because many nutrients such as vitamins and enzymes are very sensitive and are easily destroyed by processing. As you can guess, cooking alters those nutrients.

If you go back to the basic diet of fresh raw foods, exercise, and natural health care, you will be providing your dog with enjoyment and quality of life. If you start your dog on raw natural whole foods, you will begin to notice a difference even in the first few days. After a few weeks, you will be amazed at the energy and look of your dog. Their eyes will be brighter and coats will look healthier. And both of you will be happier.

Life Energy is a quality that is found only is freshly grown, uncooked whole foods. It is a subtle force field that permeates and surrounds all living things. It is called by a number of names: Vital Force, Qi, Energy, and Aura. We all know that raw food contains more vitamins and minerals than cooked foods because cooking destroys and depletes many of the nutrients, changes the molecular structure of the food and makes it more difficult to digest. Heat also destroys the enzymes and antioxidants in the food.

Raw food contains enzymes and enzymes are energy and life. Farmers plant live seed because cooked seed will not sprout. It is dead. The life energy or enzymes are gone. Our bodies are born with a limited supply of enzymes that are used to repair the body. When we eat raw food, the body consumes the enzymes in the raw food. When we eat cooked or processed foods, our pancreas has to produce enzymes in order to digest the food, and then they are gone forever. Although the jury is still out on whether the body can replenish enzymes or not, the common belief is that it cannot. Dr. Edward Howell, a leading nutritionist, suggests that by the age of forty, we only have thirty percent of our enzymes left.

The same is true for our furry companions and the quality of the food makes a difference in your dog's health. The strength of your dog's immune system and his ability to fight off disease are determined by the type of food he eats. And this directly affects his quality of life.

Your dog's body is designed to be a carnivore and to receive needed nutrients from raw food. It amazes me when I give a puppy a raw meaty bone, and watch how she can rip the flesh off the bone and clean it and then settles down to chew on the bone. Her teeth and nails are designed to grab, rip and tear raw flesh. Her intestines are short and are designed to digest food quickly. The dog has been equipped with strong enzymes and other natural chemicals to help process the foods that they are designed to eat. If meat stays in the digestive system and becomes heated, it will putrefy and create poisons. But the dog does not have this problem due to the short intestinal tract. So, you see, your dog has been created by evolution to thrive on raw meat.

In order for you to have your dog as healthy as possible, it is imperative that he receive a diet as close as possible to what nature intended. Dogs, being carnivores, derive their primary nutrition from the consumption of other animals. It is critical to their health. Evolution designed them as a predator, and inadequate meat quantities will not sustain them.

When your dog's ancestors killed his prey, he would eat the stomach, intestines, liver, heart, and spleen first. These organ meats contained nutrients that are not stored in muscle meat and bones. The stomach and intestines would contain partly digested grains, fruits and vegetables which provided other nutrients; such are carbohydrates and unsaturated fats. These nutrients were also essential for his health. Dogs are not totally carnivores, so these other additions to their diet are absolutely necessary.

Then the dog would eat his prey's bones, fat, and muscles to complete his full complement of vitamins, minerals, enzymes, carbohydrates, proteins and fats. Later, he would eat the occasional insect for more protein and B12. After a nap, he would go looking for water. Dogs do not eat and drink water at the same time. Drinking water at the same time as eating will upset the acid-alkaline balance of the digestive system by making minerals pass through the body without being used. That certainly rules out dry processed dog food that is mixed with water to make gravy!

So, the bottom line is that a fresh raw diet is the correct diet for our wonderful dogs. Let's go to the next chapter and see just what foods are available for us to feed our furry friends.

"Let food be thy medicine."

— Hippocrates

"Water is the most neglected nutrient in your diet, but one of the most vital."

— KELLY BARTON

CHAPTER THREE

Foods to Use

Boston Terrier – Dawson

Just what foods can you feed to your dog? The answer is to go back to the basics of fresh raw whole foods. The closer you can come to providing the diet that evolution designed for your dog, the more he will enjoy good health. And you will be providing the nutrients in the form that he needs in order to thrive.

I think you will be surprised at the wide variety that is available and that is very important. By providing variety, you will not deprive him of any of the nutrients that he needs. Since our dogs are carnivores, we will start with meats and then move on to vegetables, fruits and many other things. These are the basic food groups for your dog.

RAW MEATS

This group represents the protein foods. It includes beef, poultry, lamb and rabbit. It is important to note that it includes both muscle and organ meats. Muscle meat is located between the skin and bones of the animal. The organ meats include all the organs of the animal. Feed more muscle meat than organ meat, because too much organ meat can upset the nutritional balance and also cause a loose stool. Use organically raised, free range livestock. That includes beef, poultry, lamb, and rabbit. You do not want to expose your dog to the hormones and drugs that are in typically raised livestock. It is easier to find this quality of meat these days in natural markets, whole food stores, and even many grocery store chains are beginning to carry organically raised meat. At least try to feed organ meats from organically raised livestock, because the organs filter and store some of the drugs and chemicals that are pumped into typically raised livestock. Organ meats that are easy to find are liver (chicken, turkey and beef), hearts (beef, chicken or turkey), and chicken and turkey gizzards.

If you are concerned about there possibly being bacteria content in raw meat, stop and think about what species you are feeding. Dog's digestive systems have evolved over millions of years to be short and acidic, which can handle bacteria. Also their system is designed to get the necessary nutrients for good health from raw meat. Bacteria are not a problem for a dog with a strong immune system and a strong immune system is created by eating species appropriate raw food. And there is a lot of proof that raw meat promotes good health.

Handle raw meat as you would for yourself.
Be sure to clean kitchen surfaces and keep the meat
refrigerated. When cleaning your kitchen surfaces, be
sure to use natural cleaning products, because you do
not want to poison your dog with chemicals.

Raw eggs are a good thing to add to the meat a few times a week. Some vets feel that it is all right to feed the raw white and yolk, while others feel that you should feed only the raw yolk. The debate centers on whether raw egg whites can cause a biotin deficiency. I feed only raw egg yokes, but you may check with your own holistic veterinarian and see what her view is. And be sure that you are using no-hormone, no-drug eggs from free range chickens. They contain higher omega-3 content than eggs from caged hens.

Raw meat and eggs provide an array of species-appropriate nutrients and they are all in a form of bioavailability. HERE IS A LIST:

* Amino Acids   * Fatty Acids

* Phosphorus   * Antioxidants

* Folic Acid
* Potassium
* Biotin
* Inositol
* Protein
* Calcium
* Iodine
* Selenium
* Choline
* Iron
* Sodium
* Chromium
* Magnesium
* Sulfur
* Coenzyme Q10
* Manganese
* Vanadium
* Copper
* PABA
* Zinc
* Enzymes
* Pantothenic Acid
* Vitamins A, C, D, E, K, B1, B2, B3, B5, B6, and B12

I buy meat for my dogs from a natural whole food market. I get chicken necks and turkey necks from them. I always have them grind some of the chicken necks so that I can feed it with vegetables and supplements, etc. They are also kind enough to package them into one or two pound packages for me. I have a meat grinder at home to grind larger cuts of chicken, such as leg quarters, or whole cut up chickens and grind organ meats in with it. My dogs get muscle meat and bone along with the other food groups that I mix in. I also package it in portions that will feed my dogs two or three meals, and then place them into the freezer.

Feeding meat in ground form allows you to mix in other ingredients, such as eggs, vegetables, fruits and supplements. It is also important to feed your dog chunk meat and I will cover this subject under Raw Bones next.

RAW BONES

This is the most fun food you can give to your dog. There is nothing that my dogs love more than a meaty bone. They each find their own place, settle down, and stay there for hours, first pulling all the meat off the bone and then chewing on and eating the bone itself. The puppies stand on the bone and pull the meat off. This is excellent exercise for their neck, back and jaw muscles. The meat is providing all the nutrients listed above and the bones are giving them calcium.

You must always feed a bone RAW! When a bone is cooked the molecular structure changes and that causes it to splinter. It can cause serious problems for your dog.

Do not ever feed a cooked bone to your dog.

Raw edible bones, on the other hand, provide excellent nutrition in a natural form for your dog. It provides good upper body and intestinal exercise. It is also excellent for keeping your dog's teeth clean. Edible bone is a bone that your dog can totally consume.

Raw poultry bones with meat on them are good for your dog. As I said, RAW, because cooked poultry bones will splinter and present a problem. But your dog can chew and crunch up raw poultry bones very easily. Since I have toy dogs, I feed them chicken necks and sometimes small turkey necks, and will also grind up a whole chicken, so that they get the muscle meat of the chicken along with the rest of the bones.

Larger dogs can also eat backs, legs, and whole quarters of chicken and larger turkey necks. A large dog may also enjoy an occasional whole chicken. The great thing about necks is that they are full of edible cartilage. If your small dog handles a chicken neck well, you may also feed a chicken wing. If they do not eat all the bone, be sure to pick it up and throw it away because when it dries out, it can splinter.

You may notice that some chicken necks have a lot of skin and fat attached to them. Raw fat is good for your dog, but too much may cause them to fill up quickly and not eat the rest of their meal. Just pull off some of the extra fat so that they do not get too much. I feed two or three chicken necks at a time to each dog, and I leave the skin and fat on one and pull the skin off the others.

If you know someone who hunts see it you can talk them out of some venison ribs or ground venison for your dog. My dogs love a venison rib and you can feed ground venison just as you would any other ground meat.

You can also buy beef ribs for your dog. Buy some with enough meat on them to provide a meal or a good snack. I like to have them for rainy days. They give the dogs hours of entertainment. Buy ribs that are the right size for your dog. I get short beef ribs for my toy dogs. If you have a large dog, be sure you get bones large enough that they can chew, but not small enough that they may try to swallow whole.

Also, if it is the first time to give your dog a bone, stay close and observe and see how he handles it. If he does not eat the complete bone, you may want to throw it away if it has become small enough that he may swallow it. I have never had a dog choke on a bone, but then, I never want to give them the opportunity.

RAW MEATY BONES CONTAIN:

* Marrow   * Amino Acids

* Antioxidants   * Protein

* Fiber   * Enzymes

* Essential Fatty Acids   * Minerals

* Vitamins

RAW VEGETABLES

First of all, be sure to use organically grown vegetables. They have a higher nutrient content, and have not been treated with dangerous chemicals. Many large grocery chains are beginning to carry organic items, and of course you can get them at whole food and health food stores. With organic vegetables you can be sure that the produce has not been dyed, waxed or irradiated. If you have to use non-organic produce, be sure to wash it thoroughly. You can use a bit of dishwashing detergent, or one of the fruit and vegetable rinses that are sold in stores. But definitely organic is better.

Even though your dog is a carnivore, she still needs the nutrients that are found in vegetables. And she will thrive best on ground up vegetables. Remember that the digestive tract is short, and does not have time to utilize the nutrients in vegetables if they are fed whole. That is why you want to grind them up. You can do this with your food processor. One exception to this is that many dogs like to get a whole raw carrot and eat it as they would a bone. The chewing action is good for the teeth and gums. My dogs like whole carrots as a treat.

Vegetables come in two main groups – those that grow above ground and those that grow below ground. It is good to use items from both groups in the same meal.

THE ABOVE GROUND VEGETABLES ARE:

Broccoli – It's one of the best sources for calcium, potassium, and fiber. You can use the buds, leaves and stems. My dogs love broccoli, and when I am cutting up a head, they are dancing around the kitchen, and when I feed them pieces, it turns into a broccoli frenzy!

Brussels Sprouts – They are related to both the cabbage and broccoli families. They contain vitamins K, A, C, B6, and B1, manganese, potassium and protein.

Cabbage – Cabbage is high in vitamins C, E, iron, folate, beta-carotene and potassium. Dark green leafy cabbage is better.

Cauliflower – It is low in sodium and high in fiber, vitamin C, potassium, and zinc. The green leaves are very nutritious. Cauliflower contains less folate and beta-carotene than broccoli and cabbage.

Broccoli, Brussels Sprouts, Cabbage, and Cauliflower are members of the brassica family, and they contain

phyto-chemicals like glucosinolates which are
proven to reduce cancer.

Asparagus – Asparagus is the leading vegetable to provide folic acid. Folacin is necessary for blood cell formation, growth, and the prevention of liver disease. It is low in sodium, but high in carotene and vitamins C and B6. It also contains potassium.

Corn – Cut fresh corn off the cob. Corn contains beta-carotene, vitamins B and C, protein and fiber. Be sure that the corn is fresh and tender.

Okra - Okra is also known as Gumbo and Lady's Fingers. It is a high-energy Food and contains vitamins A, B-complex and C, folic acid and calcium.

Squash – The squash family consist of summer and winter squash. Summer squashes are yellow squash, patty pan and zucchini. Winter squashes are acorn, butternut, carnival and hubbard. Summer squash is tender and you can put all of it, stem included, in the food processor. Winter squash has a hard shell that needs to be peeled off first. Squash is highly nutritious and contains protein, calcium, iron, magnesium, manganese, phosphorus, potassium, vitamins A and C, folate, and zinc.

Pumpkin – Pumpkins have a sweet taste and your dog will really like it. They have beta-carotene, vitamins A, C and E, folate, niacin, calcium and more.

Peas - Peas are high in magnesium. They have vitamins A and C, iron and protein. Use green peas, snow peas and sugar peas.

Green Beans – Green beans are high in protein, potassium, iron, thiamine and vitamins A, C, and K.

Greens – Greens consist of collard greens, bok choy, kale, mustard greens, swiss chard, spinach, and beet greens. Greens contain vitamins A and C, iron, folate, magnesium, calcium and lutein. Avoid feeding a lot of spinach, Swiss chard, and rhubarb, because they contain oxalic acid that interferes with calcium absorption.

Tomato – I know, I know…it's a fruit. But most people think of it as a vegetable.

They are rich in vitamins A and C, folate and potassium.

THE BELOW GROUND VEGETABLES ARE:

Carrots - Carrots are the leading source of beta-carotene.

Sweet Potatoes – They contain large amounts of beta-carotene and other carotenoids. They also contain vitamins A, C, B6, E, copper, potassium, iron, and manganese. Be sure to use the peel.

Yams – Often confused with sweet potatoes, yams are seldom sold in the US. However, their nutritional value is the same as sweet potatoes.

Turnip Roots – Turnip roots are easy to find during the winter months, when many other vegetables are hard to find. They are full of nutrients, and they do not have to be peeled before you put them into the food processor.

The main thing to remember is to feed a variety of vegetables and change the combinations every few days, and that way you will not be feeding too much of one thing at a time. Be sure to prepare them in a digestible form by putting them through a food processor or blender. And feel free to use vegetable parts that you would normally throw away, such as stems and tops. There are a few vegetables that you should not feed your dog, and I have them listed in the section Foods To Avoid.

FRUITS

Dogs have a sweet tooth, just like we do. You can feed fruits to you dog as a treat between meals, and there are some that you can mix with their vegetables. The same things apply to fruits as to vegetables. Just be sure to buy organically grown in order to get the additional nutritional value and avoid waxes, chemicals, insecticides and irradiation. Fruits are great for vitamins, minerals and vital energy.

There are a few fruits that you should <u>not</u> feed your

dog, and I have listed them in the section

Foods To Avoid.

Only feed one fruit family at a time and feed it on an empty stomach. It can go through the digestive system quickly, in twenty or thirty minutes. Most, when fed with a meal, stay in the digestive tract too long and tend to ferment. After feeding fruit as a snack, be sure to wait at least thirty minutes before you feed your dog a main meal. Your dog will like dried as well as fresh fruits. Just be sure that you feed unsulfured and organic. Be careful of feeding too much because of the sugar content and if they are dry and sugary, do not use them.

Apples – All varieties. They are a rich source of pectin, which is a soluble fiber which removes toxins, lowers cholesterol and reduces the risk of heart disease. They are also a good source of vitamin C. This is one of the fruits that can be mixed with the meat and vegetables, and the sweetness enhances the taste of the food.

Avocados – They are filled with nutrition. Avocadoes contain vitamins A, C, E, C and B-Complex, phosphorus and magnesium. They are a good source of fruit oil.

Pears – All varieties. Pears are an even better source of pectin than apples. They are also a good source of potassium. Dried pears contain protein, iron, and vitamins A and C. Pears can also be added to the meat and vegetable mix.

Bananas – They are highly nutritious and are high in potassium, magnesium, vitamin B6, and folic acid. Be sure that they are ripe with a yellow skin with brown specks. Under ripe bananas are difficult to digest.

Berries – You can feed your dog just about any berry. As with any fruit you are eating, just give them a bite and see if they like it. Berries are rich in fiber, iron, magnesium, phosphorus, potassium, vitamins A and C, selenium, calcium and folate. Two of my dogs love blueberries and one does not care for them.

Citrus - Oranges, tangerines, grapefruit, lemons and limes. These fruits are high in vitamin C. I have never had a dog that would get near citrus fruit. But, if your dog likes citrus, it is ok to feed it to him. Be sure to feed the white membrane just under the peel because it contains bioflavonoids which are needed to absorb vitamin C. I have fed my dogs the membrane when I am eating citrus.

<u>**Do Not Feed**</u> **the peel** *of citrus fruits -*

it is poisonous.

Peaches, Apricots, Nectarines – They are high in vitamins A and C, contain calcium, niacin, potassium, contain fiber and are low in saturated fat, cholesterol and sodium. Be sure to remove the pit or stone from these fruits before you feed them to your dog.

Figs – All figs are high in nutrition and contain iron, potassium, beta-carotene, benzaldehyde, flavonoids, and a digestive enzyme called ficin.

Just a reminder, dried figs are five times higher in calories than fresh figs.

Plums – They are a good source of potassium and contain vitamins A and E.

Dates – Dates are high in iron and potassium and have amounts of folate and vitamin A and the B vitamins.

Mango – Yes, my dogs love mangos. They are rich with beta carotene, potassium, magnesium, vitamins C, B1, B2, B3, and B6, and zinc, iron and calcium.

Melons – They're a great source of vitamin A and C and potassium. But because they are mostly water, they go through the digestive system very quickly.

They are excellent organ cleansers, especially for the kidneys. You might want to feed this as a treat in the mornings.

So, the next time you are eating a piece of fruit, offer some to your dog and see if she is interested. You just may be surprised.

FATS AND OILS

Fats and oils are what really provide the energy for your dog. In fact, they provide more than twice as much energy as other food sources. They are necessary for the growth and maintenance of many of the tissues in your dog's body, and they naturally reduce inflammation in the body. They provide support for healthy skin, hair, joints and the heart.

The fatty acids are smaller components of fat and they are necessary for good health.

Omega-6 Fatty Acid - Linoleic acid is required for dogs and it is found in fresh foods in the natural diet. When it is present in the diet, your dog can produce whatever other fatty acid that is required. Omega-6 is found in safflower, sunflower, corn, evening primrose and borage oils, and it is also in poultry fat.

Omega-3 Fatty Acid - Linolenic acid is found in canola and flax oils, flax seed and walnuts. It also includes fish oils, coldwater fish, like salmon, mackerel, halibut and herring. I think salmon oil from the North Atlantic Sea is the best, such as Norwegian Salmon Oil. Another source is eggs that are from free-range chickens. They have a higher content of omega-3 than eggs from cage raised chickens.

You can purchase EFA's at a health food store in the refrigerated case. Be sure to get organic oil that is unrefined, and keep it refrigerated at home. Heat, light and oxygen can turn them into trans-fatty acids and that is dangerous for your dog's health. Hemp seed oil contains a balance of both omega-3 and omega-6 oils, and flax seed oil also contains both, but more of the omega-3.

The fatty acids are important and without the proper amount in the diet, it can lead to many health problems. Deficiencies are common and the less severe symptoms are a dull, dry coat, itching and scratching, greasy skin, skin infections, and excessive loss of hair. More severe problems are skin that doesn't heal, liver and kidney damage, heart and circulatory problems, and a suppressed immune system.

WATER

Water is the most abundant and the most important nutrient found in the body. Since approximately two-thirds of a dog's body weight is water, then it is very important to provide the best quality water for your dog.

Water is involved in nearly every body process. Think about it. It is involved in digestion, circulation, absorption and elimination, making it the primary source of transporting nutrients throughout the body.

Good quality water is absolutely necessary for your dog's health. Be sure to use a glass or stainless steel bowl. Do not use a plastic or aluminum bowl and ceramic bowls may contain lead. Have water available for your dog at all times, inside and outside the house. Wash the water bowl everyday to avoid dirt and contaminants.

Do not use tap water. City water is known to not only contain fluoride, but may also contain many other toxins, such as pesticides, lead, nitrates, cadmium, sodium, arsenic, asbestos, insecticides, fungicides, herbicides, benzene, dioxin and toluene. (Makes you wonder why we drink it!) Many of these are known to cause cancer, and others can damage the liver, brain, kidneys, and cardiovascular system. Many medical tests have shown that fluoride may cause cancer. If you have your own well water, it may not be any safer, so be sure to have it checked often.

Provide pure drinking water for your dog. Use distilled or reverse osmosis water. You may also notice that your dog begins to drink less water once he begins the raw food diet. That is because raw food contains a lot of moisture and becomes a natural source of liquid for your dog.

EXTRAS

Extras are just that - just a little something extra for your dog as a treat.

Raw Seeds and Nuts - This is something that you may not have thought of. But they must be raw and unsalted. They are high in fat and can become rancid in the heat, so be sure to keep them in the refrigerator. Do not feed peanuts or peanut products, because they may contain aflatoxin, a carcinogen. Also, do not feed alfalfa seeds.

Plain Goat Yogurt - Another favorite is plain goat yogurt. You can find it at the health food store or whole food market. You can feed it by itself as a treat, or mix it in with a meat meal. Goat milk yogurt is best for dogs, because it is higher in fatty acids than other milks. It is a natural antibiotic and is high in acidophilus, a beneficial bacteria, which aids in digestion.

NUTRITIONAL SUPPLEMENTS

Feeding a well balanced, fresh raw diet will provide most of the vitamins and minerals that are needed by your dog. But as her guardian, it is good to know about nutritional supplements to make sure that all the bases are covered.

Bonemeal – is the only supplemental form of calcium that is complete and safe for dogs. You can purchase it at a health food or whole food store and it is sold in a powder form. **<u>Do Not</u>** purchase bonemeal that is sold at garden supply stores which is **<u>never</u>** to be used as a food. Mix it with fresh raw meat. The raw meat will stimulate acid in the digestive system and that aids in the calcium absorption. If you have a large dog, it is important to feed bonemeal, especially if they have bone or hip problems. One tablespoon per one pound of meat is sufficient for the average dog.

Aloe Vera – This is a wonderful product that has many uses, but at this time, I will only be addressing how it benefits the digestive tract. You can purchase aloe vera juice or gel at a health food store. Get certified organic that used some form of vitamin C as a preservative. The label may identify the vitamin C as citric acid or ascorbic acid. The label should also state that the bottle contains a minimum of 99 percent pure aloe vera. It may also contain potassium sorbate which is a mold inhibitor. Be sure to keep it refrigerated after it has been opened. Aloe vera is also excellent for colitis, constipation, diarrhea, indigestion and helps in detoxification.

THE AMOUNT OF ALOE VERA TO ADD TO EVERY MEAL:

Two teaspoons for small puppies and tiny dogs

One tablespoon for large puppies and small dogs

Two tablespoons for dogs 20-40 pounds

Three tablespoons for dogs 40-60 pounds

Four tablespoons for dogs 60-80 pounds

Five tablespoons for dogs 80-100 pounds

Six tablespoons for dogs over 100 pounds.

Do Not give Aloe Vera to pregnant females, as it can overtax their system.

Vitamin C - is good for maintaining collagen which is necessary for the formation of connective tissue, ligaments, muscles, tendons, skin and bones. It helps form adrenalin that is needed for stress, fights bacterial infections, and is needed in forming red blood cells. It stimulates the immune system and enables the body to resist diseases. Depending on your dog's size, he should receive 500 to 8000 mg per day. Purchase vitamin C in a powder or crystal form.

Bee Pollen – is a natural supplement and contains protein, vitamins, minerals, enzymes, carbohydrates and micronutrients. It can be given every few days.

Purchase bee pollen in granules and give one-quarter teaspoon to small dogs, one-half teaspoon to medium dogs and one teaspoon to large dogs.

Garlic – Use garlic to increase intestinal health. It helps eliminate worms, and strengthen digestion. It is also good for dogs that are overweight or have hip pain. You can include fresh, grated garlic with each meal. Use ½ clove for dogs 10-15 pounds; 1 clove for dogs 20-40 pounds; 2 cloves for dogs 45-70 pounds; 2 ½ cloves for dogs 75-90 pounds; 3 cloves for dogs 100 pounds and over.

Coconut Oil – is used as a preventative for the flu and it is excellent in preventing infection. It kills most strains of the flu virus, and when taken daily, it is effective against the canine flu. Coconut oil comes in a solid form in a jar. The recommended dose is one teaspoon per 10 pounds of body weight daily. It works best in divided doses given two or three times per day. Most dogs will eat it off the spoon. Ex: Give your 30 pound dog one teaspoon in the morning, one teaspoon later in the day, and one teaspoon at night. One of the doses can be mixed with her meal.

Prozyme – is a natural plant enzyme food supplement. It helps to breakdown foods and aids in the digestive process so that your dog can get more nutrition from her food. It also helps if your dog has a gas problem. It is very helpful in older dogs to help them get the most nutrition possible from their food.

Colostrum – is excellent for immune support, and is very good to give to your dog when he is at risk of a fungal, viral, or bacterial infection of the gastrointestinal system. Be sure to get bovine colostrum from New Zealand from organically raised cattle. Colostrum is the "first milk" from the mother after birth and contains all the immune support that an offspring needs. Since cows produce more than can be consumed by a calf, the excess is collected and put in a powder form for supplement use. You should give your dog 500 mg of colostrum per 25 pounds of body weight once or twice a day, depending on your dog's risk factor. It is also excellent in helping to fight dog flu.

I cannot leave out the importance of **Vitamin D**. This is the sun vitamin and the best way to get this is from the sun. Be sure that your dog has plenty of time outside so that he can soak up the sun and air. If she is an inside apartment dog, be sure that she has a window that has sun and raise it so that she gets the direct sunlight. And try to take her out as often as you can. If you are lucky enough to have a fenced yard, be sure that your dog

stays outside for long periods of time, weather permitting, and that they exercise at least two hours a day. I cannot believe the difference in my dogs since I fenced my backyard. They run and play, bark and chase, they are very happy and they bring that happiness indoors with them. I cannot express too much the importance of fresh air and sunlight.

As you can see, there are plenty of foods available for you to mix and match so that your dog should not become bored with one food. Of course, even with the changing around that I do, I never see my dogs hesitate to eat. They always dive in and act as if they have not been fed for weeks. This is good. They are healthy and happy, bright eyed and energetic and love to run and play. Isn't that what you want for your dog?

"Come forth into the light of things,

Let Nature be your teacher."

— WILLIAM WORDSWORTH

CHAPTER FOUR

Foods To Avoid

Boxers – Java and Cammi

Since nutrition is the foundation to your dog's health, you want to feed the best diet possible. I for one believe that the whole foods raw diet is the best. It consists of raw, organically raised meats and organic fruits and vegetables. By feeding this quality food to your dog, you will improve his health, and extend the length and quality of his life. But along with knowing what is best to feed your dogs, you must also be aware of what NOT to feed your furry companions.

The old saying is true – you are what you eat. If you feed poor quality dog food to your dog, his digestive system will bear the consequences. The organs that are affected are the liver, pancreas, kidneys and skin. The liver and pancreas are affected as part of the digestive system and the liver, kidneys and skin as part of the elimination system. The most damaging thing about the majority of dry commercial dog foods on the market today is that they contain toxic dyes, chemicals and preservatives. Those toxins build up in the body and over time cause damage to the liver and kidneys.

The number one killer of dogs today is cancer. In 1997, oncologists from Colorado State University's College of Veterinary Medicine published diet recommendations to help combat cancer. Since cancer cells thrive on sugar and create lactate as a waste, they recommend excluding fluids that contain milk and/or sugar. The lactate poisons the dog by depleting its energy, making it weaker. So, limit sugars and simple carbohydrates. A diet that can meet the anti-cancer recommendations is a homemade species appropriate diet. That diet is the whole raw foods diet.

THE 1997 STUDY ALSO PROVIDED KNOWLEDGE OF SOME OTHER FOODS TO AVOID.

Chocolate – I hope that you already know to never, never, NEVER feed your dog chocolate. It contains theobromine, which is toxic for your dog. It also contains caffeine which is a nerve irritant. Your dog can go into a coma and die from eating chocolate.

Sugar – Sugar in whatever form, is addictive, causes damage to the pancreas, and depletes the body of vitamins and minerals.

Dairy products – Milk has foreign hormones and lactose, which is a sugar. Most dogs do not have the lactase enzyme that is needed to digest lactose.

Grain – Dogs do not need the carbohydrates in grains for nutrition and energy.

Fats and protein in a natural dog diet provide the fuel that your dog needs. Grains break down into sugar in the body and they can also add to many health problems. They can cause your dog to have skin allergies, hot spots, bloating, ear infections, joint problems, and digestive disorders. Some vets believe that they weaken the immune system and the pancreas.

Raw Salmon – Be careful in feeding salmon. In fact, it is better and safer to give your dog Norwegian Salmon Oil. Salmon poisoning is an infectious disease caused by a parasite fluke on salmon. Although it is mostly found in Pacific salmon, it can occur elsewhere.

Onions – Raw or cooked, one quarter cup of onions can make a 20 lb. dog sick.

Onions cause toxicity by oxidizing hemoglobin in the red blood cells. When this happens, it forms clumps in the red blood cells which prevent them from carrying the oxygen that is needed. These small clumps are called Heinz bodies and when veterinarians see them, they strongly suspect onion toxicity. The signs of onion toxicosis are the same as anemia and low oxygen in the body – lethargy, weakness, red urine, decreased stamina, and pale or bluish gums.

Raisins and Grapes – Can cause toxicity in dogs. Some dogs may never be affected, but for the ones who are, it is best to avoid feeding to any dog. Some dogs will develop kidney damage within the first days of eating grapes and/ or raisins, which can lead to kidney failure and death. So, it is in the best interest of your dog to avoid this food altogether. If your dog should accidentally eat grapes or raisins and have a reaction to them, their first reaction will be vomiting. Get them to a Vet immediately in that if they are treated early, they can recover. At this time, it is not known what the toxin is.

Macadamia nuts – They are toxic to dogs and create hind limb weakness, tremors, depression, vomiting and fever. Dogs usually recover.

Moldy food – Dogs can have indiscriminating taste, as we know. And moldy food can produce tremor syndrome that can result in seizures.

Peach pits – The pits and seeds of most fruits are toxic to dogs. Signs of poisoning are drooling, vomiting, and lethargy. If you suspect that your dog has eaten a peach pit or pit or seed of any fruit, take him to the veterinarian as soon as possible.

Bread dough – A ball of dough can obstruct your dog's gastrointestinal tract.

Also, the yeast can ferment in your dog's stomach and cause signs of ethanol ingestion or drunkenness.

I hope that this has helped raise your awareness that not all foods that may be good for you are appropriate for your dog's health. Many can cause very severe health problems. By avoiding potentially dangerous foods, and providing healthy foods, you can add to the quality and joy of your dog's life.

"Nobody can be in good health if he does not have fresh air, sunshine, and good water."

— Flying Hawk, Oglala Sioux Chief

CHAPTER FIVE

Putting It Together:
RECIPIES AND PORTIONS

American Bulldog

In order for the body to heal itself, we must provide the best nutritional support possible. Because veterinarians get little education in nutrition, and are courted by the major manufactures of commercial dog food, you cannot always rely on their recommendations.

But the main thing that we need to take into consideration is that each dog is an individual and his particular nutritional needs must be considered. The best way to know if you are meeting your dog's nutritional needs is by observing him and noticing how he responds. It may take a month or two to see the response to a change in diet. It may take three to six months in some dogs and with a very ill dog, it may take a year. But don't give up. Remember that the main reason you're doing this is for the health and longevity of your beloved dog.

A homemade fresh food diet is as close as you can come to a natural diet for your dog. Using raw meat and bone, organic vegetables and fruits, and a few supplements to balance the diet can make a good substitute for freshly killed prey. Some dogs can handle small amounts of grain and it may be good for them. But for so many, grains are not needed and may cause allergies. This is where your dog as an individual must be considered. And this is where your dog will be your best guide to the proper diet for her. Your dog should have a healthy, shiny coat and be energetic and glow with life. This is what the raw diet can do for her.

If you can not feed fresh raw food all the time, then give it as often as you can. It is better to give your dog what you can, even if it is just a few meals a week, then to not feed her a natural diet at all. But I think you will see in Chapter 6 that there are some alternatives to help you feed your dog the best diet possible.

MAKING THE CHANGE

Most dogs take to the new diet right away, but some may need some time to adjust. If you have always fed commercial processed food to your dog, it might be best to introduce the diet gradually for a seven to ten day period. Mix the ingredients of the raw diet and combine about a fourth of a serving with a three-fourth serving of the usual food that your dog eats. Over several days, increase the amount of the raw diet and decrease the amount of the old diet, until your dog's diet is made up of 100% of the raw diet.

During this change, you will want to add a digestive enzyme for dogs to her food. This will help replenish enzymes and increase friendly intestinal flora. One product you can buy is called Prozyme. You can purchase this product from a veterinarian or on line. Ask your local health food store, but be sure that you do not try to use a digestive enzyme for humans.

Once your dog has made the change over to the raw diet, she may try to make up for vitamin deficiencies by eating more than usual. But after those are met, you will notice that she will eat less of the new food than she did commercial food. That is because the raw diet is meeting her nutritional needs.

You may even notice that the stool volume and consistency will change. That is because the nutrients in the raw diet are high in bioavailability for your dog. The stools tend to be more firm and are easier to clean up as well as being more biodegradable. You can help control the consistency of your dog's stools by adding more stool-firming or stool-loosening foods. The above ground vegetables, oils, fats, and vitamin C are usually loosening. The below ground vegetables and bones tend to be firming.

After your dog goes on the new diet, you may also notice other differences. By finally eating a healthy raw diet, your dog's body can begin to do some healing or "detoxing." Some dogs will never show any signs of detoxing, but depending on the number of years your dog has been on commercial dog food may decide how much of the process the body needs to go through.

Detoxification is a natural healing process that you should support. The digestive system needs to eliminate anything that may be harmful to the body in any way that it can. It gets rid of the toxic build up that has occurred, and leaves the body cleaner and healthier. Some of the signs that you may see are bad breath, mucus and/or parasites in loose stools, discharges from the nose or eyes, pustules or rashes on the skin, dirty ears, and body odor.

Your dog may lose a lot of dead hair because the skin is becoming active and getting ready to grow healthy new hair. The more toxins that are in your dog's body, the more intense the detoxification will be. This process can take place over a period of a few days to a few weeks. But don't be alarmed, your dog's body is getting cleaner and healthier.

You can help your dog feel better during this time. If his skin has a rash, you can bath him everyday during this period to wash the discharges away. You can also rinse him with Aloe Vera juice which will be soothing and healing. Also, adding Aloe Vera juice to his food will help heal, clean, and settle the digestive system.

If your dog has a deep underlying condition that has been suppressed by drugs, it may surface again. This would be a good time to start working with a holistic veterinarian who will use herbs, homeopathy, or some other natural remedy to help you heal your dog.

But the first step must begin with the diet, and I hope you know by now that medications and vaccines do not heal, they only suppress. Getting your dog onto the natural raw diet is the very first step in the process of healing.

PREPARING THE MEAL

Right now you may be feeling like this is going to be a lot of trouble. But, I assure you that once you get into the swing of it, it is no trouble at all. I suggest you write some recipes down and plan what you will prepare for a week, have your menu in the kitchen so that you know what you are going to prepare each day. If you go to Chapter 10 you will find a form you can use. Very soon, you will not have to look at it. And always remember why you are doing this. This is for the health of the dog that you love so much and who gives you so much more in return. Be sure that you prepare and serve his meal with lots of love and assure him that this food is wonderful and good for him.

How much should you feed your dog? That will depend on the size, breed, age, and level of activity. A toy breed will not require as much as a large breed. One of the most reliable methods is to feed an amount that seems appropriate. If your dog leaves food in his bowl, then feed a lesser amount next time. If he gobbles it up and looks to you for more, then add more next time. And be sure that you monitor his body weight. If he is gaining weight, cut back. If he is losing weight, then increase the amount. You should be able to feel your dog's ribs when you rub his sides. If you can't feel them, then he is carrying too much weight. If you can see your dog's ribs, then he needs to gain weight.

You can pulp the vegetables ahead of time. I use a food processor and grind a below and an above ground vegetable, such as a carrot or sweet potato, and zucchini or one of the squashes. Then I may add one of the dark leafy veggies and place it all in a bowl. Sometimes I add a banana or apple, then mix it all together and put it in a covered container for the refrigerator.

Putting the meal together is really very simple. Get all your ingredients together including the dog dish or dishes. Measure the meat, vegetable mix, and other ingredients into each dish and then mix together. Since the meat and vegetables will be cold from the refrigerator, I run some hot water in the sink, and then place the bowls into the water for a few minutes. Just be sure that the water does not top over into the bowls. This will warm the food, but not make it hot to destroy the oils that you added. You want to warm the food to room temperature so that it will be easy for your dog to digest. Cold food takes longer to digest and can cause some stomach upset. Do not microwave your dog's food and do not store it in aluminum foil.

Near the end of Chapter 2, I talked about the dog in the wild hunting and devouring the prey animal. Always keep that model in mind when you are preparing your dog's meal.

DOG'S WEIGHT: 10 LBS.

A. If you are using ground meat with ground bone in it:

1. **Raw Meat:** From ¼ to 1 cup meat/bone mixture

2. **Vegetables:** ½ to 1 Tbl.

3. **Kelp/Alfalfa powder:** 1/8 to 1 tsp.

4. **Vitamin C:** 500 – 1,500 mg

5. **Flax Seed Oil:** ½ tsp.

6. **Aloe Vera juice:** 1 – 2 tsp.

7. **Coconut Oil:** 1 tsp. daily per 10 lbs. of body weight

8. **Prozyme:** ¼ tsp. per 1 cup of food

9. **Bee Pollen:** ¼ tsp.

B. If you are using ground meat without bone in it, be sure to add 1/8 tsp. of **bonemeal** per ¼ cup of meat.

C. If you want to feed **Raw Bone** along with the ground meat, just cut back on the ground meat/bone mixture, and feed 1 to 2 whole chicken necks for dessert after she eats her ground meat.

D. Be sure to add a raw egg yolk per dog at least three times a week. Add one tablespoon of plain goat yogurt per dog three times per week. And be sure that you have added organ meat to the meal.

DOG'S WEIGHT: 50 LBS.

A. If you are using ground meat with ground bone in it:

1. **Raw Meat:** From 1 to 2 cup meat/bone mixture

2. **Vegetables:** 3 Tbl.

3. **Kelp/Alfalfa powder:** 2 tsp.

4. **Vitamin C:** up to 3,000 – 6,000 mg

5. **Flax Seed Oil:** 2 tsp.

6. **Aloe Vera juice:** 3 Tbl.

7. **Coconut Oil:** 1 tsp. daily per 10 lbs. of body weight

8. **Prozyme:** ¼ tsp. per one cup of food

9. **Bee Pollen:** 1/2 tsp.

B. If you are using ground meat without bone in it, be sure to add 1/2 tsp. of bonemeal per 1 cup of meat.

C. If you want to feed **Raw Bone** along with the ground meat, just cut back on the ground meat/bone mixture, and feed 1 turkey neck or 4 to 6 whole chicken necks for dessert after he eats his ground meat.

D. Be sure to add a raw egg yolk per dog at least three times a week. Add two tablespoon of plain goat yogurt per dog three times per week. And be sure that you have added organ meat to the meal.

DOG'S WEIGHT: 100 LBS.

A. If you are using ground meat with ground bone in it:

1. **Raw Meat:** From 2 to 4 cup meat/bone mixture

2. **Vegetables:** ¼ to ½ cup

3. **Kelp/Alfalfa powder:** 1 Tbl.

4. **Vitamin C:** up to 6,000 – 7,500 mg

5. **Flax Seed Oil:** 1 1/2 Tbl.

6. **Aloe Vera juice:** 6 Tbl.

7. **Coconut Oil:** 1 tsp. daily per 10 lbs. of body weight

8. **Prozyme:** ¼ tsp. per one cup of food

9. **Bee Pollen:** 1 tsp.

B. If you are using ground meat without bone in it, be sure to add 1/2 tsp. of bonemeal per 1 cup of meat.

C. If you want to feed **Raw Bone** along with the ground meat, just cut back on the ground meat/bone mixture, and feed 2 or 3 turkey necks for dessert after he eats his ground meat.

D. Be sure to add a raw egg yolk per dog at least three times a week. Add three to four tablespoon of plain goat yogurt per dog three times per week. And be sure that you have added organ meat to the meal.

E. Many people with large dogs use a combination of the raw diet and one of the dry foods that are mentioned in Chapter 6. A friend of mine has Labradors and they are fed a chicken quarter in the morning and get 1 cup of a top quality dry food at night.

Another plan that you may want to use is to feed the mixed meal four or five days per week without meaty bones, and then feed a meaty bone meal one or two days per week. A meaty bone is a bone that has plenty of meat on it. I feed my Papillons, who weigh four to six pounds, three or four chicken necks each for a meal. Also, depending on how much meat is on the bones of a beef short rib, I will feed them one or two for a meal. Then they have the bones for several days to enjoy chewing and exercising their jaw muscles, cleaning their teeth, and massaging their gums.

After your dog has eaten, it is an excellent time for her to rest. Since I have three dogs, and usually one or two more that are boarding, I feed my dogs in crates, that way they can feel safe about not having to defend their food from another dog. Also, they can eat at their own rate, although usually the first one is finished before I can get the last one into their crate. Then they can settle down and take a nap for thirty or forty-five minutes, because they should not exercise right after eating. Then I place them outside to give them a chance to socialize, run, play and do their business.

Another thing that may be new to you is that it is important to fast your dog for at least one day per week.

FASTING

If your dog is one year of age or older, it is important for them to fast one day per week. A young dog between six months and one year can fast for a half day per week. If your dog is ill, do not force him to fast, but most dogs will fast automatically when they are not well.

Fasting is a very normal thing for dogs. Fasting once a week allows the digestive system, vital organs and glands to get rest, heal, and restore themselves. It gives the body a chance to eliminate any toxins that are present.

In the wild, carnivores devour their prey quickly and eat as much as they can possibly hold. Then they rest and it may be one, two or three days before they eat again. Because their systems are designed for the gorge and fast cycle, it gives their body plenty of time to rest and purge itself.

Remember, your dog still has a digestive system like the carnivore in the wild, so it is important to allow that period of rest and rejuvenation. It is very important to give their system a break and allow their body to get rid of mucus buildup and toxins. It is very healthy for them as it is part of the natural cycle.

FASTING CONSIDERATIONS

1. I suggest that the fasting day be a day that you are at home most of the day.

2. Only healthy adult dogs eating the raw diet or fresh food diet should be fasted.

3. Be sure that your dog gets plenty of fresh air and exercise to help with the cleaning process.

4. Do not give vitamins or food supplements during fasting.

5. You may offer chicken or vegetable broth at the meal time during fasting. Do not use a broth with salt. You can make your own easily by boiling meat and/or vegetables in water and using the liquid from the broth. Then use your vegetables and meat for a stew for yourself.

6. You may give Aloe Vera juice during the fast, either by itself or in a broth. It is great in helping with the cleaning and healing process that is going on.

7. A raw bone with very little or no meat on it is a great way to keep dogs entertained.

8.   Urine and stools may be more frequent and more potent.

9. If your dog is on commercial processed food, drugs or medication, do not fast her.

10. Have a positive attitude about fasting and know that you are doing one of the things you can to help keep your dog healthy.

11. Mealtime is a special time for your dog, so on fast day, be sure to give her plenty of attention and affection at that time.

12. If for some reason you do not feel comfortable about fasting your dog, then don't do it. But it is a very natural and healthy thing to do.

SOME WORDS OF SUPPORT

Again, this may look like a lot to handle, but just remember why you are doing this. And I promise you that after you have prepared these meals for awhile, you will suddenly find that you are putting them together without even thinking. Just be sure to vary the meats and vegetables so that the diet is complete.

I thaw out enough meat to last two or three days, grind up some vegetables for the same amount of time, mix them together and keep them in the refrigerator. Then as I prepare each serving, I add the extras and supplements. It only takes a few minutes and as a result, my dogs are beautiful, happy, and healthy. And <u>that</u> is the reward.

To help you with your important Journaling effort, you will find some forms in Chapter 10 that you may print. They will help you keep tract of what you are doing. Do not hesitate to use them and make as many copies as you need. I would suggest that you put them in a binder, so that you have a history and record of your progress.

If you keep a record of what you are feeding, you will have a guideline of what your dog ate, what he liked, maybe what he didn't like, and if he had any type of reaction to it. An example would be if his stool is too loose, you can check how much vitamin C and above ground vegetables you fed to him and give him less in the next meal.

You will also find it a valuable record if you ever have to make a visit to the vet. You will truly be a responsible dog guardian. And I know you really love your dog, because you are reading this to learn how you can help her stay healthy.

"The greatness of a nation and its moral progress can be judged by the way its animals are treated."

— GANDHI

CHAPTER SIX

When You Can't Feed Fresh Food

Chihuahua - Prue

I think you realize by now that feeding fresh, whole, organically raised, natural food to your dog is the best possible diet. After all, feeding a raw diet to your dog is not a new fad, but actually a return to the dog's not-so-long-ago past. Dogs were thriving on raw meat, bones and table scraps just a hundred years ago.

But what if sometimes your work schedule does not permit you to prepare a natural meal? Of course, you can always prepare meals on the weekend and then package them into serving sizes and place them in the freezer.

I think you also have become aware that the traditionally processed dog foods on the market be they canned or dry, are not the best thing to feed your dog and could actually be harmful to her.

Well, the good news is that some of the dog food manufactures have also taken the health of our furry friends to heart, and are providing some acceptable, nutritious, raw, organic food products. This provides the convenience of prepared food and a biologically suitable food for your dog. And they have also been tested to contain all the nutrients that are needed.

RAW FROZEN FOODS

This category is the closest thing to preparing your dog's food yourself. You will not receive the variety of vegetables and supplements as you would if you prepared it yourself, but compared to traditional commercial food, it is way ahead of the game. As with preparing raw food in your kitchen, be sure to use safe food practices with these raw food products.

They contain raw muscle meat, organ meat, bones, fat, and connective tissues and some have vegetables and supplements. Some contain grain, but most do not. The best of these meat-based products meet/or exceed the nutrient profiles set for canines by the Association of American Feed Control Officials (AAFCO). They also set the standard for dry and canned foods, but because these frozen raw products are not cooked, they contain the heat-sensitive nutrients in their ingredients and do not require the addition of vitamins and minerals to be classed as "complete and balanced."

Be sure that there is raw bone included in the product, and if it does not have it, be sure that it contains an adequate substitute for calcium and other minerals. Most of these products do contain ground raw bones. That way they contain the nutritional value, but avoid any hazards that might be posed by whole bone consumption. Again, I have toy dogs and they have never had trouble with a raw bone of the appropriate size.

The North American Raw Petfood Association (NARPA) was founded in 2005, and its membership is made up of the manufactures of raw pet food. They joined together because of the assaults on their industry by the conventional pet food interest. Their purpose is to prove what advocates of the raw food diet already know, and that is that complete and balanced raw diets can produce and maintain super-healthy, well-adjusted dogs.

Most of the producers of the raw food diets are careful to have information and the nutritional breakdown of their products on the packaging. Do not buy any product that does not include this information. Too much information is much better than not enough information to help you make a choice.

The top manufactures state that they use USDA inspected and USDA passed meats. This means that the meats are human quality meats. Some state that they use totally organic ingredients, and that they use sources of meats that were grass-fed, or free of antibiotics and growth hormones. You want to purchase the best quality ingredients that you can afford.

These frozen products come in a variety of packaging — patties, tubes and containers. They should have a complete listing of their ingredients and be sure to read them. Many state that they provide a "complete and balanced diet" because they contain a single protein source of muscle meat, ground bone, vegetables, fruit and supplements like kelp and flaxseed.

Some of the other statements that you want to see are: "free range chicken," "without antibiotics or hormones," and a list of the vegetables, fruits and supplements that are used. Some products are "meat mixes," "vegetable mixes" or "organ blends" only, and you need to mix them together. Other supplements that you might see are eggs, garlic, parsley, honey, apple cider vinegar, salmon oil, cod liver oil and others.

As well as chicken, turkey and beef, some manufactures offer buffalo, quail, ostrich, Cornish game hen, rabbit, lamb, goat, wild venison, whitefish and duck. Some of the vegetables and fruit that you will see are carrots, kale, yams, sweet potatoes, and apples.

Now, where can you find these wonderful products? Most health food stores, whole food markets, and similar stores are carrying these types of frozen products. And hopefully you are near one so that you can take your product straight home and put in the freezer.

If you are not lucky enough to be near one of these retailers, then you have the option of ordering the product from the manufacturer. Most companies ship on a particular day of the week, and do overnight or two day delivery, packed in dry ice and/or a cooler. You need to arrange to be at home to receive the package or perhaps have it sent to your office if there are kitchen facilities there. Be sure that you know the manufacturers policies regarding delays and shipping mishaps, and who will pay for the meat if it arrives thawed. You certainly don't want your dog to eat it, if that is the case.

SOME OF THE TOP MANUFACTURERS OF FROZEN RAW

FOODS, IN ALPHABETICAL ORDER, ARE:

A Place For Paws
800-354-4216
www.aplaceforpaws.com

Amore Pet Foods
604-273-8577
www.amorepetfoods.com

Animal Food Services
800-743-0322
www.animalfood.com

Aunt Jeni's Home Made 4 Life
301-702-0123
www.auntjeni.com

BarfWorld
866-282-BARF
www.barfworld.com

Bravo Raw Diet
866-922-9222
www.bravorawdiet.com

Celestial Pets
818-707-6331
www.celestialpets.com

FarMore
866-507-8255
www.farmoredogfood.com

Grandad's Pet Foods
209-368-3025
www.grandadspetfoods.com

Halshan
888-766-9725
www.halshan.com

Natural Balance Pet Foods
800-829-4493
www.naturalbalanceinc.com

Nature's Menu
866-333-3729
www.naturesmenu.com

Nature's Variety's Prairie
888-519-7387
www.naturesvariety.com

Oma's Pride
800-678-6627
www.omaspride.com

Pepperdogz
866-866-3649
www.pepperdoz.com

Primal Pet Foods
866-566-4652
www.primalpetfoods.

Raw Advantage
360-387-5185
www.rawadvantagepetfood
.com

Steve's Real Food for
888-526-1900
www.stevesrealfood.com

**Three Cheers Raw!
Raw! Raw!**
330-549-3077
www.threecheersrawrawraw.com

If these brands are not available to you, but others are, you should be able to evaluate the quality of the product with the knowledge that you have learned. And of course, you can always check the ingredients with your holistic vet.

Be sure to look for products that meet your dog's needs. Does it contain certified organic foods? Does it state that it is "complete and balanced", or contains supplements? Does it contain grains or not, and what types? As well as checking with your vet, you can also discuss your dog's health status with a company representative of the dog food manufacturer. They can recommend which of their products best fits your dog's needs.

WET DOG FOOD

Most wet dog foods come in cans and some come in pouches and trays. They come in a number of forms, from a "stew" to a "loaf." The moisture content can vary greatly. All wet dog foods are heat-sterilized after the container is sealed. The process "cooks" the food, coagulates protein, gelatinizes starches, and kills any pathogens.

The foods final form dictates the category in which the manufacturer places it. You will see products described as "meat in jelly (the most expensive form)" or "meat in gravy." You want to see products that contain chunks of animal meat in a sauce that has been thickened with locust bean gum, carrageenan, xanthan or a similar gelling product or gum.

Some products list the meat as "meat analog," which is meat that is finely ground and then shaped into chunks. The chunks may be made of animal meat only, or combined with cereal. Products listed as "loaf," contain a lot of grain and are the least expensive of the wet food items. Sometimes the "loaf" will contain chunks of meat.

If you buy a product that has large chucks of poultry or fish, including their bones, don't be alarmed. The bones are fine. The canning process causes the bones to soften and they are very digestible. More of the manufactures are including vegetables, fruit and herbs in their products and they are listing them on the contents label.

SOME OF THE TOP MANUFACTURERS OF WET DOG FOODS,

IN ALPHABETICAL ORDER, ARE:

Advanced Pet Diets, Avo-Derm and Pinnacle
Breeder's Choice Pet Food
800-255-4286
www.breeders-choice.com

Artemis
Artemis Pet Foods
800-282-5876
www.artemispetfood.com

Azmira
Azmira Holistic
Animal Care
800-497-5665
www.azmira.com

California Natural, Innova, Innova Evo
Natura Pet Products
800-532-7261
www.naturapet.com

Canidae
Canidae Corporation
800-398-1600
www.canidae.com

Drs. Foster & Smith
Drs. Foster & Smith
800-826-7206
www.drsfostersmith.com

Eagle Pack
Holistic Select
Eagle Pet Products, Inc.
800-255-5959
www.eaglepack.com

Entrée For Dogs
Three Dog Bakery
800-487-3287
www.threedog.com

Evanger's For Dogs
Evanger's Dog & Cat
Food Co., Inc
800-288-6796
www.evangersdogfood.com

Evolve and Triumph
Triumph Pet Industries,
Inc
800-331-5144
www.evolvepet.com
or triumphpet.com

Lamaderm and
Natural Life
Natural Life Pet Products
800-367-2391
www.nipp.com

Merrick
Merrick Pet Care
800-664-7387
www.merrickpetcare.com

Natural Balance,
N.B. Eatables
Dick Van Patten's
Natural Balance
800-829-4493
www.naturalbalanceinc.com

Newman's Own Organics
Newman's Own Organics
800-865-2866
www.newmansownorganics.
com

Neura Meats
and **Wellness**
Old Mother Hubbard
800-225-0904
www.oldmotherhubbard.
com

Nutro Natural
Choice Ultra
Nutro Products Inc.
800-833-5330
www.nutroproducts.com

Performatrin Ultra
Peton Distributors, Inc
800-738-8258
www.performatrinultra.com

Pet Promise
Natural Pet Nutrition
800-874-3221
www.petpromiseinc.com

Precise Plus
Precise Pet Products

888-4precise
www.precisepet.com

Solid Gold
Solid Gold Health
Products for Pets, Inc
800-364-4863
www.solidgoldhealth.com

Verus
VeRUS Pet Foods, Inc.
888-828-3787
www.veruspetfoods.com

By Nature Organics
Blue Seal Feeds, Inc.
800-367-2730
www.bynaturepetfoods.com

PetGuard Organic
PetGuard
800-874-3221
www.petguard.com

Prairie
Nature's Variety
888-519-7387
www.naturesvariety.com

Sensible Choice
Royal Canin USA, Inc.
800-592-6687 (US)
800-527-2673 (Can)
www.sensiblechoice.com

Spot's Stew

Halo, Purely for Pets

800-426-4256
www.halopets.com

Blue Buffalo
The Blue Buffalo Co.
800-919-2833
www.bluebuff.com

Fromm Four Star Nutritionals
Fromm Family Foods
800-325-6331
www.frommfamily.com

Lick Your Chops and
Snowbound Naturals

Healthy Pet Foods, Inc
800-821-4640
www.healthypetfoodsinc.
com

Organix
Castor & Pollux
Pet Works
800-875-7518
www.castorpolluxpet.
com

DRY DOG FOODS

The quality of the ingredients is the key and some of the top dog food manufactures are working toward having the best in their products. Along with that, they also have good packaging, storage and educated employees. They are committed to vigilance over their product from start to finish.

The majority of the conventional dry processed dog food on the market today is of very poor quality and composed of poor ingredients. But thankfully, there are some top companies who are producing quality products.

A fresh, balanced home prepared diet made up of a variety of fresh organically raised meats and organic fruits and vegetables is certainly the best diet for your dog. But a commercial diet made of the same ingredients is far better then the typical processed dog food on the market today.

SOME OF THE TOP MANUFACTURERS OF DRY DOG FOODS, IN ALPHABETICAL ORDER, ARE:

Artemis

Artemis Pet Foods
800-282-5876
www.arteimispetfood.com

Azmira
Azmira Holistic
Animal Care
800-497-5665
www.azmira.com

**Bench & Field Holistic
Natural Canine**
Bench & Field Pet Foods
800-525-4802
www.benchandfield.com

Back to Basics

Beowulf Natural Foods
800-219-2558
www.beowulfs.com

Blue Buffalo
The Blue
Buffalo Company
800-919-2833
www.bluebuff.com

Burns

Burns Pet Nutrition
877-983-9651
www.bpn4u.com

**by Nature BrightLife,
Nature Organics**
by Nature Pet &
Animal Feeds
800-367-2730
www.bynaturepetfoods.
com

Canidae

Canidae Corp.
800-398-1600
www.canidae.com

California Natural, Innova, Innova Evo and **Karma Organic**
Natura Pet Products
800-532-7261
www.naturapet.com
and karmaorganic.com

Canine Caviar
Canine Caviar Pet Foods
800-392-7898
www.caninecaviar.com

Cloud Star Kibble
Cloud Star Corporation
800-361-9079
www.cloudstar.com

Drs. Foster & Smith
Drs. Foster & Smith
800-826-7206
www.drsfostersmith.com

Eagle Pack Holistic Select
Eagle Pack Pet Foods, Inc.
800-255-5959
www.eaglepack.com

Evolve
Triumph Pet Industries, Inc.
800-331-5144
www.evolvepet.com

Evanger's Super Premium
Evanger's Dog & Cat Food Co.
800-288-6796
www.evangersdogfood.com

Firstmate Dog Food
Taplow Feeds

604-985-3032
www.firstmate.com

Foundations and **Go! Natural**
Petcurean Pet Nutrition
866-864-6112
www.petcurean.com

Fromm Four Star Nutritionals
Fromm Family Foods
800-325-6331
www.frommfamilyfoods.com

Hund-N-Flocken and
Mmillennia
Solid Gold
Health Products
800-364-4863
www.solidgoldhealth.com

Lifespan,
Petguard Organics
PetGuard
800-877-738-4827
www.petguard.com

Merrick Pet Foods
Merrick Pet Care
800-664-7387
www.merrickpetcare.com

Newman's Own Organics
Newman's Own Organics
800-865-2866
www.newmansownorganics.
com

Organix
Castor & Pollux Pet Works
800-875-7518
www.castorpolluxpet.
com

Lick Your Chops,
Snowbound Naturals
Healthy Pet Foods, Inc.
800-821-4640
www.healthypetfoodsinc.com

Life4K9
Life4K9 Pet Food Corp
770-399-3100
www.life4k9.com

Natural Balance
Organic Natural
Balance Ultra Premium
Dick Van Patten's
Natural Balance
800-829-4493
www.naturalbalanceinc.com

NutriSource
KLN Enterprises
800-525-9155
www.nutirsourcedogfood.
com

Royal Canin Veterinary
Diet, and **Royal Canin**
Natural Blend
Royal Canin
800-592-6687
www.royalcanin.us

Performatrin Ultra

Peton Distributors
800-Pet-Valu
www.performatrinultra.
com

Pinnacle
Breeder's Choice
Pet Foods
800-255-4286
www.breeders-choice.com

Premium Edge

Premium Edge Pet Foods
800-977-8797
www.premiumedgepetfood.
com

Timberwolf Organics
Yukon Nutritional Co
863-439-0049
www.timberwolforganics.
com

VeRUS
VeRUS Pet Foods, Inc.
888-828-3787
www.veruspetfoods.com

PHD Viand
Perfect Health
Diet Products
800-743-1502
www.phdproducts.com

Prairie, Raw Instinct

Nature's Variety
888-519-7387
www.naturesvariety.com

Prime Life Plus
Owen & Mandeville
Pet Products
888-881-7703
www.ompetproducts.com

Ultra Holistic Nutrition.
Nutro Products, Inc.
800-833-5330
www.ultraholistic.com

Addiction Foods
Addiction Foods Pte Ltd
65-6227-8813
www.addictionfoods.com

Wellness and Wellness Simple Food Solutions
Old Mother Hubbard
800-225-0904
www.oldmotherhubbard.com

Wenawe
Della Natura Commodities
866-936-2393
www.wenawe.com.uy

Wysong
Wysong Corporation
800-748-0188
www.wysong.net

Zinpro
Lincoln Biotech
800-253-8128
www.lincolnbiotech.com

THESE ARE THE THINGS TO LOOK FOR WHEN YOU ARE BUYING DOG FOOD, WHETHER IT IS FROZEN, WET OR DRY:

• Buy products that do not contain artificial colors, flavors, or preservatives. You want the food to be high in animal proteins and not need added flavors.

• You want products that do not contain sugar or any other sweeteners.

• Look for foods that don't list "meat or poultry by-products." You want to buy a quality product that contains "whole meat." It has probably been handled appropriately because it is more expensive for the manufacturer.

• Do not buy a product that does not identify fat or protein by species. Just saying "animal fat" or "meat protein" is language for low-quality ingredients of uncertain origin.

• You want to use products with whole meat, fish or poultry listed as the first ingredient. It would be great if it is also listed as the second and third ingredient as well. Ingredients are listed in order of how much is in the total product.

• Look for "whole" vegetables and grains. Pick "rice," not "rice bran, rice flour." Pick "oats," not "oat bran or oat flour."

• Try to buy a product with "broth" listed versus "water." Broth has nutrition because it is the result of cooking meat, fish, or poultry parts, bones, or muscle tissue.

• Pick a product with little or no grain. Your dog does not need carbohydrates in her diet. As stated earlier, grains found their way into dog food because they were less expensive to use than meat.

• Look for the manufacturer's contact information, a toll free number, a web-site address, and a mailing address. You may want to order some of their product literature.

• See that it says **"certified organic ingredients."** Manufacturing locations have to go through additional inspections and have to meet the organic manufacturing standards in order to have that on their label. Your dog will be much better off if you can cut out any chemicals and pesticides and using products that are "certified organic" will help.

• You may find a statement that the food has passed an AAFCO feeding trial. Or possibly one of the manufactures other products has passed a feeding trial. Feeding trials are designed to see if the food is palatable and if it performs in the manner that it claims. Does it help overweight dogs lose weight, does it help puppies grow, or does it help an adult dog maintain its health?

• See if the caloric content is listed. This could help you make a decision on whether this is what to feed your overweight dog.

• Check and see if they list more than the "guaranteed analysis." State and federal laws require that the following be listed on dog food labels: the minimum level of crude protein, crude fat, crude fiber, and maximum level of moisture. Anything else that is listed is subject to testing and enforcement, so if the manufacturer lists more ingredients, it means that they have confidence in their product.

• You want to locate a "date or product code" that is easy to find and interpret. This can help you with freshness, and if there is a problem, it will help the manufacturer to trace the product.

• If you see "AIB Certification" listed, it means that the company has paid for a voluntary inspection of their plants by the American Institute of Baking. The AIB sets the standard and inspection requirements for grain-based food production.

• If a company list "APHIS Registration" on their products, it means that they can provide the registration numbers of their meat suppliers, which were assigned by the United States Department of Agriculture's Animal and Plant Health Inspection Services. This is confirmation that they are using top quality meat sources.

Expect to pay more for these products. For that reason, you may find that preparing your dogs diet in your kitchen may suit your situation better. Plus you can have that real hands-on feeling of preparing meals for someone you love. After all, he is part of the family.

The cost of the natural diet, whether you prepare it or purchase a product already put together, may cost a little more, but on the other side, you will find that your vet bills are going down. Your dog will be healthier and it will be well worth it.

Be sure to see how your dog adepts to a new food regimen. Keep a record of what you feed her and what type of reaction she may have. What you want to see is a dog who begins to have more energy, starts acting younger, whose eyes are brighter, and whose skin and coat are in better condition.

If your dog does not thrive on the food you are feeding her, than change her diet to something else.

You now have enough information to help you pick the right diet for your companion.

"To sit with a dog on a hillside on a glorious afternoon

is to be back in Eden, where doing nothing

was not boring — it was peace."

— MILAN KUNDERA

CHAPTER SEVEN

The Importance of Journaling

Chocolate Labrador Retriever Puppy

How do you like the quote above? Well, that is mostly what this chapter is about — **"being"** with your dog. This is the joining of souls. You want to notice and observe, have your hands on, and play with your dog. All of these things will contribute to his health.

You will find a form in Chapter 10 to use for your Journal. This Journal is for you, the guardian, so that you can keep notes of the observations you make and the care that you give. You can keep your Journal daily or at least every few days. This is a way to examine your dog, note changes in her physical and emotional condition, and keep a record of what you feed her. It is also a joyful way to keep a diary of the wonderful things that you see your dog doing.

No one knows your dog better than you do.

You should give your dog a good physical exam every week. You can check her whole body from nose to tail and be able to notice if anything has changed. No one knows your dog better than you do. And using the exam outline below will help you get use to the normal feel of her body. Just as with the diet, after you have done it a few times, it will become second nature to you and not take much time. Having your hands on your dog is also a great way to strengthen the bond between the two of you.

This is the best way to stay on top of any problems that may occur. Although I think you will find out over time, that your dog will be so much healthier, there will be fewer visits to the veterinarian. It is still a good idea to have a veterinarian give your dog a physical once a year.

THE EXAM

Nose: Look at both the right and left nostril and check for any discharge. If it is clear and appears on occasion, that is alright, but an ongoing discharge is a sign of a problem, such as an allergy. A thick discharge is abnormal and is an indicator of a bacterial infection of the sinuses or nasal cavity. Feel for air coming from both nostrils to be sure that there is no obstruction in the nostril. The nose can be wet or dry and should be black or pink. If the end of the nose is red, you can apply Aloe Vera until it clears up.

Eyes: As you examine the eyes, there should not be any matter in the corners. If there is a discharge, pull down the lower eyelids and see if the tissue is red or inflamed. The tissue is called the **conjunctiva** and should be pink. If it is inflamed and producing white or greenish discharge, then it is a case of conjunctivitis. One home remedy is to make a cup of strong black tea. After it is cooled, place three to four drops in the affected eye three times a day. The tannin in the tea has anti-inflammatory and antimicrobial properties. Make the tea fresh each day.

The surface of the eye should be clear and the **pupil** should respond to light and both should be of equal size. The **lens**, behind the pupil, should be clear, but if it appears cloudy, it may be a sign that cataracts are beginning to form. It could also be a sign of diabetes. The white of the eye, the **sclera**, should be white. If there should be a problem with the liver, it will become yellow. The **eyelids** should be smooth and not have any bumps. Sometimes older dogs develop benign tumors on the eyelids.

Ears: The tissue on the inside of the outer part of the ear is called the pinna. It should be flat and light pink in color. If it thickens, it could be indicative of an ear infection, an allergy or a blood blister. Look into the canal and it should be clean and free of any discharge. If there is a small amount of light yellow wax, that is normal. If there is a heavy amount of wax or an odor, then there may be an infection. You need to clean your dog's ears right away.

You can use Aloe Vera juice or a 50/50 mixture of vinegar and water as cleaning solutions. Hold the tip of the ear, drop 5-6 drops of the solution into the canal and massage the base to loosen the debris. Use a soft tissue or cloth to wipe the excess liquid from around the ear, but do not place anything down into the canal. Your dog will shake his head and throw the debris out. You may need to repeat this several times over several days. If you should happen to notice a tick or other foreign body in the canal, have your holistic veterinarian remove it.

Mouth: The **lips** should be smooth and show no signs of inflammation. If your dog is a large breed with lip folds with lots of extra skin, be sure to pay extra attention. If there is a lot of saliva accumulation, clean the area with a mild medicated antiseptic.

Lift the lips to inspect the **teeth**. Be sure to look at the molars in the back as well as the teeth in the front. There should be forty-two teeth in a dog. Are they white or are they dark and covered with a brown deposit? None of the teeth should be cracked or broken and none of the roots should be showing.

The **gums** should be a healthy pink color. If you see any redness along the teeth, or any bleeding of the gums, then this is a sign of gingivitis and your dog may need his teeth cleaned. Ask your holistic veterinarian for any home remedies.

Feet: Check your dog's feet for any foreign matter between the pads. Be sure the **pads** are free of any cracks, cuts or sores. Check the **nails** to be sure that they are the right length and are not torn or ragged. Nails that are too long can cause a dog to have difficulty walking and when they start to split, they can become caught on things and tear from the foot.

Coat: A healthy coat should be soft and shiny and not greasy or too dry. If your dog is a long hair breed, you should brush her everyday, or at least every other day. Brushing her coat encourages the hair to grow and the coat to breathe. It allows you to remove dead hair and any foreign items that have made their way into the coat. Brushing is good for the circulation of blood in the skin of both long and short hair dogs, and this is healthy for both the coat and the skin. This is an excellent time to examine your dog for ticks or fleas. Run your fingers through her coat and then smell your fingers. If you smell an unpleasant or fishy odor, it may be a sign of poor health. This is another good reason to be on the raw diet.

Skin: The skin is the largest organ of your dog's body, and is a good indicator of what is going on in the body. If she has dry, flaky skin, than you need to add more flax oil into her diet. If you see areas or patches of hair loss, than you may be dealing with a skin condition. Here again, if you are feeding the raw natural diet, I doubt that you will ever see any of these conditions.

Be sure to take note of any lumps or bumps that you might feel. Record it in your Journal and keep a record on the size, if it is soft or hard, if it moves or not. If any lumps are hard, fast growing, and not easily moveable, be sure to check with your vet right away.

Vital Signs: Check your dog's **pulse** rate and blood pressure. The best place to check is inside your dog's back leg. Put your three middle fingers across the middle of the inside thigh and press moderately. You should be able to feel the femoral artery. This can be more difficult with small dogs. The pulse should be strong and regular. If it is too strong, it may indicate high blood pressure. Count the number of pulses in fifteen seconds and multiply by four to get the number of beats per minute.

Pulse Ranges for Healthy Dogs

Small dogs should have 90 – 120 beats per minute.

Medium dogs should have 70 – 110 beats per minute.

Large dogs should have 60 – 90 beats per minute.

The average **temperature** for your dog should be 100.5 F – 101.5 F (38.0 C). If your dog has a temperature of 103.5 F (39.5 C), he is running a fever. The way to take his temperature is by placing a thermometer in his rectum. The thermometer should be almost clean when removed, but if there is blood, diarrhea or black tarry stool, it is abnormal.

Normal Temperature

The average temperature for your dog should be 100.5 F – 101.5 F (38.0 C).

The normal **respiration** rate for your dog should be 10 – 30 breaths per minute. You can watch your dog breathe to make the count and there should only be a slight rise and fall of the chest with each breath. Put your ear to your dog's chest to listen to the lungs. Listen to both sides.

They should be clear and you should not be hearing any crackling sounds.

Place your hand over your dog's heart to feel it beating. You will be able to count the number of **heart beats** per minute. The best place to feel your dog's heart is on the left side of his chest, at the 3rd, 4th, and 5th rib space, directly behind the left armpit. Listen to his heart by placing your ear directly over it. The normal sound that you should hear is a quiet lub/dub. If you hear a swish sound, it could be a heart murmur. Be sure to have your veterinarian check it out.

Musculoskeletal: Now is the time for you to focus on your dog's muscles and bones. This is the system that helps her move. Start at the neck and run your hands along the spine all the way to the tail. Notice if the muscles have any unusually firm or knotted places in them. Message any tight muscles and make a notation in your Journal. Your dog will love having a massage of the lower lumbar muscles. With your hands placed on either side of her spine, use your thumbs to make deep circular motions with moderate pressure. Work on any affected areas once a day for five minutes at a time.

Next you want to check the muscles and bones in the legs. Starting with the toes, use moderate pressure to each of the joints and move them back and forth. Notice if there is any discomfort to your dog in the elbows or shoulders of the front legs or in the knees or hips of the back legs. Be sure to make a note if she shows any resistance to moving them.

Stools: You should always make note of the appearance of your dog's stools as much as you can. Be sure to note if there is anything unusual about them. Note if there is any blood or parasites present.

Genital: If you have a male dog, examine the sheath of the penis to be sure there is no abnormal discharge. With a female, be sure to check the skin folds of the vulva for any infections. If there is an infection, wash the area with an antiseptic and apply Aloe Vera cream.

Urine: Be sure to check urine on occasion, to be sure that there is no blood or mucus in the urine. If there is, it is a sign of a possible bladder infection. A home remedy is using vitamin C and cranberry juice. The vitamin C dose should be 250 mg per 20 pounds given daily.

Lymph Nodes: There are some lymph nodes and a salivary gland located at the bottom corner of the jaw and the beginning of the neck. They are also located in the area in front of the shoulder blades and behind the knees in the rear legs. If any of the lymph nodes are enlarged, it can be a sign of a local or general infection, or it can be an early sign of cancer. Anytime your feel an enlargement, be sure to take your dog to your holistic veterinarian.

EXERCISE

It is very important that your dog has exercise everyday. The best times of the day are early morning and in the evening. He should not exercise immediately after a meal. I let my dogs rest for thirty or forty minutes before I let them out again. It is also good for him to exercise in all types of weather, except in the full heat of a summer day. Dogs need abundant daily exercise in order to digest their carnivorous diet. It is important for blood circulation and to strengthen the organs of the body. The lungs, veins, and arteries will weaken in strength as the years go by. His coat will become dull because the blood circulation will not be sufficient to feed the coat.

Be sure that you record the amount of time your dog exercises, or the walk you take with her, or the dog park you can go to. Remember that exercise is just as important as feeding her.

Use your Journal to write down any concerns that you have and the plan that you have to make a difference. Be sure to note the changes that you see, both good and bad. Having all this information will prove invaluable to you in caring for your dog. And be sure to record those antics and funny things that you see her do, that make you laugh.

"When the minds of the people are closed

and wisdom is locked out,

they remain tied to disease."

— HUANG-TI, 2696-2598 B.C.

(FROM THE NEI CHING SU WIN, OLDEST MEDICAL BOOK EXTANT)

CHAPTER EIGHT

Looking Ahead

Lakeland Terrier

Now you know that nutrition is the very foundation of health. That is what it takes to improve, support, and have a strong immune system, which is the body's natural way to fight disease and heal itself.

So, what else is available to help you keep your dog healthy and to share a long life with her?

I've encouraged you to find a good holistic veterinarian to help you on this path with your dog. The term holistic refers to and treats a being as a whole. Every part is connected to every other part. No one part of the body stands on its own. All the parts and systems of the body are connected to each other and work together for the good of the being. It not only looks at the physical being, but also takes into account genetics, the mental and emotional state, as well as environmental factors that affect the being. It looks at the "whole" picture and what affects the "whole" being. This applies not just to humans, but to all animals.

Contemporary medicine, also known as allopathic medicine, uses treatments, drugs, vaccines, or surgery, to control, stop or suppress the expression of disease. The symptom may disappear, but the root cause of the condition is driven deeper into the body, until it expresses itself in a different way.

Holistic medicine encompasses many different disciplines. The major ones are homeopathy, chiropractic, acupuncture, and herbal therapy. There are others such as naturopathy, massage therapy, acupressure, Reike, Sshiatsu, kinesiology, and many more. All of them believe that the body has a central force that keeps it in balance, protects it from disease and allows it to heal. Many holistic veterinarians practice several of these methods.

ACUPUNCTURE

Acupuncture began in China around 4000 years ago and is still practiced today. Specific points of the body are stimulated by needles to produce a local or generalized effect. It stimulates the local tissues to respond and the blood supply to increase. As well as needles, massage, heat or even lasers may be used. Acupuncture deals with energy and balance to promote healing.

HOMEOPATHY

Homeopathy is the treatment of disease with minute doses of substances to stimulate the immune system to fight the disease on its own. The doses or remedies are matched to the symptoms. In other words, if they are given to a healthy body, they will produce symptoms that are like the symptoms of the disease. Homeopathy is founded on one basic principle, "Like is cured by like." It is known as the Law of Similars and was accepted by Hippocrates among others. Its present day form is founded on a system set up in the early 1800s by Samuel Hahnemann. It is a very pure science and is probably the most powerful of the alternative treatments.

CHIROPRACTIC

Chiropractic is one of the hands-on therapies that have been used around the world since the time of Hippocrates. It views disease conditions as a result of the misalignment of the body structure, especially the spine, and that interferes with the normal flow of the life force, nerve impulses, and blood circulation. These misalignments can cause constant pain, muscle spasms and organ problems. Stress can make your dog sick and can contribute to chiropractic problems. Fortunately, there are many holistic veterinarians who offer chiropractic services. It would probably serve us all if we would go to a chiropractor on a regular basis, not only for our health, but for the health of our dogs. We must realize that our dogs often take on our problems and our stress, as well as their own.

HERBAL MEDICINE

This is probably the oldest form of treatment. All folk medicine in every culture since ancient times have used herbs. The emphasis is on the specific use of herbal leaves, roots, and flowers to stimulate healing. Wild animals, when ill, have used these plants instinctively for eons. Herbs tend to show a slower and deeper healing action as they help the body with this process by aiding in elimination and detoxification. They can affect the body in many ways, and it is best to go to a practitioner who is familiar with both the good and bad effects.

THE NEXT STEP

The above was meant as an introduction to show you that there are many, many natural ways available to help promote your dog's health. As you can see, there are a number of treatments and cures that have always been available to us. Modern day medicine has chosen not to treat the body as a whole, but rather as a group of parts. You cannot attempt to heal one specific part without affecting the rest of the whole.

One of my great grandmothers was the "herb lady" in her area of rural Alabama. Every one who lived in the area came to her for her cures and tonics. My mother remembered going into the woods with her to help collect leaves, roots, plants and bark. Mom told me that she wished she had paid more attention. And that was just 80 years ago!

These alternative forms of medicine were actually the main types that were available until recent times. They were practiced and handed down by wise women, medicine men and healers for many thousands of years, and now they are called "alternative." I think we are beginning to see that modern pharmaceuticals have, over time, harmed us more than they have helped us.

Advertising by the giant companies have really done us and our dogs harm. The big commercial processed pet food companies and the large pharmaceutical corporations have not only convinced us, but our doctors and veterinarians, that they are right and have the only answer. Some of us are beginning to know better, and I hope that this book has helped you realize that there are other, safer, alternatives.

I will be addressing the alternative practices and cures in my next ebook, but I wanted to introduce you to them now, so that you would know that although diet and nutrition is the basis to health, there are also some additional ways to care for your dog.

"We are alone, absolutely alone on this chance planet,

and amid all the forms of life that surround us, not one,

excepting the dog, has made an alliance with us."

— MAURICE MATERLINCK

CHAPTER NINE

Conclusion

Shetland Sheepdog – blue merle – Heather

Well, here we are at the end of this book, and you are about to begin a wonderful journey with your furry friend. The information that I have shared with you is not new, it's as old as the species itself. But I hope that I have presented it in a way that makes it easy for you to feed and care for your dog, and to understand why this diet is so important and appropriate for your dog.

They are not able to go out and hunt for the food that they need, so it is up to you to provide the foods that will make them healthy and help them thrive. That is the least they deserve!

I hope you have come to realize that we are poisoning our dogs with commercial foods, drugs and medications. Our dogs are suffering from malnutrition and chronic diseases that can be prevented with the abundance of fresh and nutritious foods that are around us.

Care for your dog and network with your friends and the other people who help you care for your dog. Help educate them and ask questions as to why they are doing what they do. If feeding fresh foods bring health, happiness, and quality of life to our companions, why would they not join you in that endeavor?

Dogs are a magnificent species and it is they who chose to be with us those many years ago. They who wanted to partner with man. There is no way we could have made that happen, it is what they wanted.

The contributions that they have made to man are too numerous to count. They guard us and have gone to war with us; hunt and play with us; rescue, save and work for us; and they are therapy dogs for the infirmed and challenged. But above all, they are loyal and they love us.

We did not ask, but this is what they bring and all they want is to be with us. They are our companions, our friends, our children, and they bring us peace and calm.

By feeding them the diet that they need and treating them with the alternate methods that are available, we can help them to be healthy, happy, and increase the quality and length of their lives. As their guardians, this is what we want for them. We need to educate ourselves in these subjects, so that we are prepared to give them the best care. There are many good books on these subjects, and I invite you to become familiar with them.

The love that we have for our dogs and the love that they have for us is very special and there is no other love that compares to it. Our dogs understand us in a way that not even our best friends can begin to approach.

We are their guardians and their caretakers, although many times the roles are reversed. But it is our pleasure and our duty to care for them, and to see that they have health and quality of life. It is our privilege to make their lives the best possible while we are blessed to have them.

And we are truly blessed!

"For every disease that afflicts mankind,

there is a treatment or a cure

occurring naturally on the earth."

— DR. NORMAN FANSWORTH, PHARMACOGINIST

CHAPTER TEN

Forms

1. MENUS

2. JOURNAL

MENUS

Name: _____

Meals: _____ times per day at _____

AM/PM _____

1. Raw Meat: _____

_____

2. Vegetables: _____

_____

3. Kelp/Alfalfa powder: _____

_____

4. Vitamin C: _____

_____

5. Flax Seed Oil: _____

_____

6. Aloe Vera juice: _____

_____

7. Coconut Oil: _____

_____

8. Prozyme: _____

_____

9. Bee Pollen: _____

_____

Other Supplements: _____

_____

_____

_____

_____

_____

Comments: _____

_____

_____

_____

_____

_____

_____

_____

_____

_____

_____

_____

_____

JOURNAL

Name: ———————————————————————————

Date: ———————————————————————————

Eyes: ———————————————————————————
———————————————————————————————

Ears: ———————————————————————————
———————————————————————————————

Nose: ———————————————————————————
———————————————————————————————

Teeth/Gums: ————————————————————————
———————————————————————————————

Feet/Pads/Nails: ———————————————————————
———————————————————————————————

Coat: ———————————————————————————
———————————————————————————————

Skin: ———————————————————————————
———————————————————————————————

Body Muscle Tone: ————————————————————
———————————————————————————————

Stools: ————————————————————————————
———————————————————————————————

Type of Exercise/Length of Time: ——————————

——————————————————————————————————————

——————————————————————————————————————

——————————————————————————————————————

——————————————————————————————————————

——————————————————————————————————————

Behavior and Temperament: ——————————————

——————————————————————————————————————

——————————————————————————————————————

——————————————————————————————————————

——————————————————————————————————————

——————————————————————————————————————

Observations/Changes: ————————————————————

——————————————————————————————————————

——————————————————————————————————————

——————————————————————————————————————

——————————————————————————————————————

——————————————————————————————————————

Changes you would like to see/Plan: ——————————

——————————————————————————————————————

——————————————————————————————————————

——————————————————————————————————————

——————————————————————————————————————

——————————————————————————————————————

ABOUT THE AUTHOR

I'M SANDRA BAILEY, AND THE FIRST PET that I had was a kitten. I only had it for about a week and had to give it up because I had a severe allergy. I was told at the time that I would never be able to have a pet.

So, I had goldfish instead, the ones with the big fan tails and pop eyes. One would always be gold and the other black, and of course they were named Goldie and Blackie, but without #1, #2, etc. attached to the name.

When I was fourteen, a cocker spaniel in the neighborhood had a litter of mixed puppies looking for homes. Somehow I convinced my parents that I would be ok if I got one. I promptly picked out the runt and when Mom asked why,

I said, "Because she looked like she needed me." And that began my love affair with dogs.

I got my next dog from the Humane Society in Los Angeles. He picked me by never taking his eyes off me as I walked up and down looking at all the dogs, and he was with me for fourteen years. I discovered after he left for the Rainbow Bridge, that he had been a Papillon mix, so that is when I became involved with Papillons.

When I lost my first Papillon at the young age of nine, I began my study in nutrition and alternative health care. I felt that there was a better way to care and support our dogs, improve their immune systems and extend their lives as long as possible. I am a member of the National Center for Homeopathy and a Professional Member of the Animal Wellness Association.

I have shown Papillons for over twenty years, and have become more and more involved in various aspects of the canine world. I currently have three Papillons, but I do not breed them because I readily admit that I would not be able to part with any of them.

Since my retirement from Human Resources work in the corporate world, I have set up a doggie daycare and overnight stay in my home, Digit and Pip's Doggie Daycare. My overnight doggie guests sleep in my bedroom with me and my dogs. Where else?

I am currently working on the next book in the Naturally Healthy Dog Series, plus some articles and reports. Stay tuned.

The Author with Squeeze, Pip, and Digit at their home

in Charlotte, NC

RAINBOW BRIDGE

JUST THIS SIDE OF HEAVEN

is a place called Rainbow Bridge.

When an animal dies that has been especially close to

someone here, that pet goes to Rainbow Bridge.

There are meadows and hills for all of our special friends so

they can run and play together.

There is plenty of food, water and sunshine, and our friends

are warm and comfortable.

All the animals who had been ill and old are restored to

health and vigor; those who were hurt or maimed are made

whole and strong again, just as we remember them in our

dreams of days and times gone by.

The animals are happy and content, except for one small

thing; they each miss someone very special to them,

who had to be left behind.

They all run and play together, but the day comes when one suddenly stops and looks into the distance. His bright eyes are intent; His eager body quivers. Suddenly he begins to run from the group, flying over the green grass, his legs carrying him faster and faster.

You have been spotted, and when you and your special friend finally meet, you cling together in joyous reunion, never to be parted again. The happy kisses rain upon your face; your hands again caress the beloved head, and you look once more into the trusting eyes of your pet, so long gone from your life but never absent from your heart.

Then you cross Rainbow Bridge together....

Author Unknown....

APPENDIX

IF YOU DO NOT KNOW A HOMEOPATHIC or Holistic Veterinarian in your area, please visit these sites:

ACADEMY OF VETERINARY HOMEOPATHY

751 N.E. 168th Street

N. Miami Beach, FL 33162-2427

PHONE: 303-652-1590

FAX: 305-653-7244

EMAIL: avh@naturalholistic.com

or avhlist@naturalholistic.com

WEBSITE: http://www.theavh.org

The Academy of Veterinary Homeopathy encourages the teaching and practice of classical (Hahnemannian) homeopathy veterinarians. They maintain a list of veterinarians who are certified in homeopathy and the list is available at their website.

AMERICAN HOLISTIC VETERINARY MEDICAL ASSOCIATION

2218 Old Emmorton Road

Bel Air, MD 21015

PHONE: 410-569-0795

FAX: 410-569-2346

EMAIL: AHVMA@compuserve.com

WEBSITE: http://www.ahvma.com

The American Holistic Veterinary Medical Association encourages the practice of many holistic methods, including nutrition, chiropractic, acupuncture, and homeopathy, and others. They maintain a list of holistic veterinarians. Mail them a stamped, self-addressed envelope to receive a copy of the list.

PHOTO ACKNOWLEDGEMENTS

THE PHOTO ON THE COVER, and this photo, is of a beautiful Doberman Pinscher named Kodi. Kodi is ten years old and has always been on the natural diet. He is in excellent health. His guardian is Robin Morehouse and the photos were taken by Mary Hoggard.

FOREWORD - Ch SunBelt's Calamity Call with daughter SunBelt's Caret – photo by Sandra Bailey. Ch SunBelt's Euro – photo by Robin Morehouse

INTRODUCTION - Digit at 3 months – in the snow – photo by Julie Saunders. Ch Benjerbo Phoenix – photo by Alverson Photographers, Inc.

CHAPTER 1 - American Rat Terrier "Nipper" in a photo by Ellen Levy Finch

CHAPTER 2 - Bassett Hound Delacroix Helen's Boy With Diamondice in a photo taken by sannse

CHAPTER 3 - Boston Terrier "Dawson" in a photo by Ellen Levy Finch

CHAPTER 4 - Boxers "Java" (natural ears) and "Cammie" (cropped ears) in a photo by Ellen Levy Finch

CHAPTER 5 - American Bulldog in a photo by sannse

CHAPTER 6 - Chihuahua – photo by Chris of his dog named "Prue"

CHAPTER 7 - Chocolate Labrador Retriever puppy - photo by Ellen Levy Finch

CHAPTER 8 - Lakeland Terrier in a photo by sannse

CHAPTER 9 - Shetland Sheepdog (blue merle) – photo by Ellen Levy Finch of Marshland Fantom of the Opera, "Heather"

ABOUT THE AUTHOR - Sandra, Squeeze, Pip, Digit - photo by Christine Mullen

CONTACT INFORMATION

YOU MAY CONTACT SANDRA BAILEY AT:

info@thenaturallyhealthydog.com

sandragbailey@yahoo.com

"REAL DOGS DON'T EAT KIBBLE"
~BONUS~

I HOPE THAT YOU HAVE FOUND THIS book of value and I would really appreciate your input. I would also be happy to answer any questions that you might have. Contact me at info@TheNaturallyHealthyDog.com.

Another important thing to know in caring for your dog is CPR. To receive your Special Bonus Report of **"CPR for Dogs,"** visit me on the web at www.TheNaturallyHealthyDog.com/?id=46. This report is a $10.00 value.

Also, to help you on your way, sign up for the **"Healthy Recipe of the Week"** newsletter, worth $65.00. You well receive a healthy, safe recipe every week that will help make a difference in the health of your dog. Go to www.TheNaturallyHealthyDog.com/?id=42.

But wait, there's more.... A 15 minute phone conference with me, to answer your questions about the raw diet and to help get you started. Value $50.00. Visit www. TheNaturallyHealthyDog.com/?id=47.

Be sure to visit www.TheNaturallyHealthyDog.com and sign up for my Free Newsletter. Receive health tips and information on current issues, and it all benefits your dog.

And remember to tell your friends about this book. They, and their dog, will thank you.

Thanks!

Printed in the USA
CPSIA information can be obtained
at www.ICGtesting.com
JSHW082205140824
68134JS00014B/440

9 781600 373015